MY VISION

Challenges in the Race for Excellence

Published by Motivate Publishing

PO Box 2331, Dubai, UAE
Tel: (+971 4) 427 3000
e-mail: books@motivate.ae www.booksarabia.com

MOTIVATE

Published 2012

First published in Arabic with the title رؤيتي - التحديات في سباق التميّز

المكتب الإعلامي
THE MEDIA OFFICE

ISBN: 978 1 86063 344 7

British Library Cataloguing-in-Publication Data. A catalogue record for this book is available from the British Library.

Printed by Emirates Printing Press, Dubai

MY VISION

Challenges in the Race for Excellence

Mohammed bin Rashid Al Maktoum

To my brother,
His Highness Sheikh Khalifa bin Zayed Al Nahyan, President of the UAE and Ruler of Abu Dhabi

In appreciation of His Highness's admirable efforts to follow in the footsteps of our late founding fathers, who built a huge monument to their love for their country; and in expression of our loyalty and support for His Highness's wise leadership.

CONTENTS

INTRODUCTION

In the name of Allah, the Most Gracious, the Most Merciful

During the last ten days of Ramadan,[1] a journalist asked me, "If God blessed you with a sighting of the Night of Destiny (*Laylat al-Qadr*)[2], what would you wish?"

I was about to reply: "I wish God would promote the status and prosperity of the Emirates and its people," but after briefly hesitating and reconsidering the question for a few moments, I asked myself if I would be depriving the very people I would want to wish this for, even though my own people are closer to me than other Arabs.

The Prophet Mohammed (PBUH) once said, "None of you will be a true believer, until he wishes for his brother whatever good he wishes for himself."[3] I wish the same good for my own people as I do for all Arabs. I want them to reach the same advanced levels enjoyed by developed countries, I wish they could take initiatives, excel and make inroads in all fields. This is what we are trying to do in the United Arab Emirates in general and Dubai in particular. Although we are proud of our past achievements, we strive to accomplish greater ones. Yet, we will never feel satisfied until all Arabs prosper, achieve and excel.

I feel increasingly sad about the sorry state of affairs of the Arab world. Only a persistent sense of optimism about a brighter future lifts my sadness. I keep telling others and myself that all this despair, pessimism and fear are transient, and like a lonely cloud crossing a clear sky, will soon disappear. What unites Arabs largely surpasses their differences, but although the opposite is true for many other nations, we still see those nations heading towards unity and integration.

This constant Arab discord is not normal, because under normal circumstances, we would form a single bloc. We will never be able to achieve this if trivia dominates our major concerns and negative attitudes keep overwhelming the positive. Today's Arab crisis is not one of money, men, morale, land or resources, because thank God, these are plentiful and are backed by a large consumer market.

The real crisis is rather one of leadership, management and perennial egotism. This is the kind of crisis that is bound to happen when lust for power prevails over granting people the love and care they deserve, and when the interests and destiny of one individual become more important than those of a whole nation. This is also what happens when the interests of some groups and cliques benefiting from certain leaders are served instead of those of all the people; in other words, when you put the people at the service of the government, in sharp contrast with the norm.

As for me, I am proud of my religion, my country and my nation. I am just as proud of my leader, the late Sheikh Zayed bin Sultan Al Nahyan;[4] my late father, Sheikh Rashid bin Saeed Al Maktoum;[5] and my late brother, Sheikh Maktoum bin Rashid Al Maktoum.[6] I am also proud of my two living brothers, Sheikh Hamdan bin Rashid Al Maktoum[7] and Sheikh Ahmad bin Rashid Al Maktoum,[8] my family, the citizens of the UAE and all Arabs, everywhere.

Our distinctive development experience in the UAE is a good example of what can be done when God blesses a country with an unselfish leadership that strives for the good of its people and not its own. Good leadership puts the interests of the community as a whole before those of any specific group.

Credibility of leadership can only be established through action and not words. I am referring here to the kind of action that distinguishes a leader who considers his people his country's foremost asset, and not one who looks at them as a burden. There is a world of difference between a leadership that is based on love and respect, and one that is based on fear.

Our vision is sharp, our goals are clear, our resources are huge, our will is strong and we stand tall, ready to face the challenges ahead. Our mission is for Dubai to become an international, pioneering hub of excellence and creativity, and we are already striving to make it the world's premier trade, tourism and services destination in the twenty-first century. We are confident we can reach this ambitious goal thanks to our dedicated leadership and by providing the necessary infrastructure and environment. But even this is not enough. We also want Dubai to lead in security, safety and dynamic growth, without neglecting that all-important element of trust, which we are keen to maintain throughout the local, regional and international business communities. Dubai will never settle for anything less than first place.

All that is needed in order to reach these goals is to show our people the right direction and nurture their potential for innovation, creativity, self-confidence, determination and leadership. Those who lead from the top of the pyramid end up leading only those on top, which is not how an exclusive development exercise should be carried out.

Because development is a common and concerted effort and requires common leadership, a true leader should select leaders from the ranks of his own people. Once he selects the right leaders, they will join him in forging ahead to the final destination. As the Prophet Mohammed (PBUH) once explained, "Religion is all about sincerity." When we asked Him for whom, he replied: "For Allah, his Book, his Messenger and for the leaders of Muslims and their masses."[9]

It was also reported that Jarir bin Abdullah, a companion of the Prophet, once said: "I gave the pledge of allegiance to the Prophet for offering prayer perfectly, giving zakat[10] and giving good advice to every Muslim."[11]

I wrote this book with the aim of providing advice and explaining our experience to our Arab brethren in the sincere hope that they will find it helpful. Our commitment to help them achieve a high level of development is as strong as if we were helping ourselves. Although failure is a great teacher, we cannot afford the time to learn from our failures. Human societies cannot be subjected to such a process.

Because we are dealing with human beings, we must opt for a successful development experience and a scientific approach that can be applied in all Arab countries. We are growing in a sustainable way, entertaining ambitious development plans, moving quickly over several areas of development and learning all the time. The advice we provide should not, however, be generalized in its approach and we should never ask people to do more than is possible. Whatever we have learned so far, we have learned from trial and error. We want to share our experiences with our Arab brothers, so that they can use it on the march to the success they would wish for themselves – and which we would wish for them.

We consider the achievements of the UAE and Dubai the achievements of all Arabs. This consideration will remain foremost in all the ventures we are planning for the future. In this way, we will be providing them with all our experiences and expertise, so that they may use whatever they deem suitable. In addition, we are also offering our brotherly commitment to help them as much as possible in achieving their goals.

I am as confident that all the elements needed in a distinguished Arab development process are available, as I am about the ability of Arabs to achieve their goals. Successful development may have been a dream in the past, but that is no longer the case. This book will explain why.

– Mohammed bin Rashid Al Maktoum

---

1 The ninth month of the Islamic calendar, observed by Muslims as a month of fasting.

2 The night the first verses of the Qur'an were revealed to the Prophet Mohammed (PBUH) and prayers are accepted.

3 *Sahih Bukhari*, narrated by Mohammed Ibn Ismail Al Bukhari and freely translated from the Arabic.

4 Sheikh Zayed bin Sultan Al Nahyan (1918–2004) was the first President of the UAE and Ruler of Abu Dhabi. Together with Sheikh Rashid, he took a leading role in taking seven different emirates into the UAE Federation in 1971.

5 Sheikh Rashid bin Saeed Al Maktoum (1912–1990) was the Vice-President and Prime Minister of the UAE and Ruler of Dubai.

6 Sheikh Maktoum bin Rashid Al Maktoum (1943–2006) was the Vice-President and Prime Minister of the UAE and the Ruler of Dubai.

7 Sheikh Hamdan bin Rashid Al Maktoum (born 1945) is the Deputy Ruler of Dubai and the second son of the late ruler, Rashid bin Saeed Al Maktoum.

8 Sheikh Ahmad bin Rashid Al Maktoum (born 1950) is the fourth and youngest son of the late ruler, Rashid bin Saeed Al Maktoum.

9 *Sahih Muslim*, narrated by Muslim Ibn Al Hajjaj Al Nisaburi and freely translated from the Arabic.

10 Zakat (alms) is the third of the Five Pillars of Islam and refers to donating a portion of one's wealth to the poor and needy.

11 *Sahih Bukhari*, narrated by Mohammed Ibn Ismail Al Bukhari and *Sahih Muslim*, narrated by Muslim Ibn Al Hajjaj Al Nisaburi, and freely translated from the Arabic.

Part I

THE PULSE OF DEVELOPMENT

CHAPTER ONE

The Lion and the Gazelle

With each new day in Africa, a gazelle wakes up knowing he must outrun the fastest lion or perish. At the same time, a lion stirs and stretches, knowing he must outrun the fastest gazelle or starve. It is no different for the human race. Whether you consider yourself a gazelle or a lion, you simply have to run faster than others to survive.

Since its inception in 1971, the United Arab Emirates has flourished at an unprecedented rate – one that has astounded the world and still seems to be accelerating.

This young and dynamic country has achieved a great deal since 1971. It competes at all levels in a diverse range of sectors and leads the world in a number of trail-blazing projects. Nevertheless, there is still much to do. We are not content to rest on our laurels, basking in the glory of what we have achieved; we are constantly striving to move forward, to grasp the moment with both hands and capitalize on the opportunities presented to us in a rapidly globalizing world.

To date, our achievements have helped us catch up with the rest of the world in its drive to globalize. This process began slowly during the last two decades of the twentieth century, before accelerating exponentially in the new millennium, and can now be seen as a prelude to what is set to become the most important economic race that the world has ever witnessed. The prize is one of epic proportions and failure is not an option.

To ensure success, we have to join the race and win. After all, no one ever remembers who came second – not even the second man to climb Everest or walk on the moon!

A nation's development, however, does not happen overnight or by accident. Nor does the development of a nation ever stop once the process has begun.

Nation building is the result of intense efforts at building a community and homeland; a phenomenal task not undertaken lightly, but shouldered by a nation's government, its public and private sectors, and its people. They must all be willing to respond to the rapidly changing conditions that ricochet around the world at breakneck speed.

In order to achieve this, a modern infrastructure is not enough; we must have the vision and flexibility to embrace change, to continuously adapt, and to improve our personal performance and our commitment to service. This will enable us to expand our markets and promote our competitiveness on the international stage. Doing so requires time, dedication and hard work.

It goes without saying that the government is deeply committed to the UAE. We believe it is our duty to serve our community and embrace its aspirations, both now and in the future, by assuring our people economic growth, education, health, security, stability, comfort, leisure opportunities and freedom of movement. This will allow for the most conducive atmosphere to achieve the targets that will guarantee our welfare and a bright future. All those who work for the government must appreciate the task ahead of them and rise up to the challenge.

In order to lay solid foundations for the country's future, we must build upon the achievements forged by our founding fathers – achievements that must not stop with our generation, but must continue and be perpetuated by future generations. History shows no mercy for weaklings. Sheikh Zayed and my father, Sheikh Rashid, our beloved late leaders, never waited for history to record their feats; they were proactive in making history themselves and in doing so, set the benchmark for us to follow.

Progress and regression

In today's fast-paced world, if you are not leading, you will be left behind. If you fall behind, it is likely that someone less capable, less creative and less prepared than you will take your place. Although this can happen very quickly, the race is also one of endurance. Should you stumble once or twice, do not worry, you can learn valuable lessons from falling occasionally and will be unlikely to repeat the same mistakes. Failure is not falling to the ground; it is remaining there once you have fallen and the greatest failure is when you decide not to stand up again.

The UAE's leadership fully understands that if our country lags behind others economically, it will be left behind. It also knows large-scale development will not only improve the country's physical infrastructure, but eliminate unemployment, ignorance, poverty and illness.

When nations fail to develop, they become vulnerable to a collapse in security and stability, and lose the foundations on which their prosperity was built. They also risk being subjugated to tyranny and prejudice, and after a few years of recession, lose most of the benefits, status and respect they had acquired over several decades of development.

Before I assumed my position as the country's Vice-President and Prime Minister, and Ruler of Dubai, I also served as the UAE Minister of Defence and am well acquainted with the ravages of war. War does not provide solutions or put an end to problems, but rather the opposite. Our world is far from ideal and wherever we look, we will find countless examples of suffering, even in our own region. We can speak of war as vehemently as some others do, but because we believe otherwise as Muslims, we prefer to speak of peace. When we greet people or say goodbye, we say *assalaam alaykum* (peace be upon you).

The secrets behind a nation's greatness do not lie in its military clout. Contemporary history is littered with examples of nations made powerful by their military forces but which, in reality, are powerless because of their fledgling economies. Conversely, there are nations with small military forces that are economic superpowers. Nations can only overtake other nations through economic and not military power, as testified by history.

We Arabs have a rich military past. Our faith in God and our determination to overcome other nations of the time led us to expand our influence. We managed to accomplish some of the greatest military victories the world has ever known and in the process, became the greatest power on earth.

But the power of nations ebbs and flows in rhythmical cycles and it was inevitable that our nations would weaken and gradually deteriorate, until nothing was left of our previous glory but our heritage.

Dissecting our illustrious past reveals that Arabs were not just a superior power in terms of military prowess. We were also an economic and maritime superpower of the same calibre as the Phoenicians, Greeks and Romans in ancient history; Europe in modern history and more recently, the United States of America.

When Abu Jafar Al Mansur[1] was looking for the right place to build the capital of the Abbasid dynasty, he did not select Baghdad, the city of peace, because it was impregnable and easily defended or suitable for use as a springboard to wage war on other nations. He chose Baghdad for the simple fact that it straddled the commercial and maritime crossroads of the time.

He said to his aides, "This is a good site for a city. The Tigris River is here and there is nothing hampering the way to China, which supplies us with all the goods we need by sea, while our staple foods can be obtained from the Jazeera region and Armenia. The Euphrates River, on the other hand, will bring us all we need from the Cham and Riqqah regions and their surrounding areas."[2]

Today the economy remains the same as it was in the past and will be in the future – the nerve centre of life. The economy is a nation's bread and butter; its stability, prosperity and politics; and the essence of mutual relations and interests between nations. The presence of all these factors at any one time may spark the creativity of some people and lead them to pursue their visions. This is how civilizations are built.

Although many civilizations never survived long enough to leave a lasting impression on history, some assimilated their ideas with those that preceded them, and enjoyed periods of development and excellence. This also happens when the people of a nation blend into a working team, or when God endows them with an open-minded leadership, that in turn, gives developers and creators free rein to create something unique. This is the formula for building civilizations – the one that has provided the blueprint for the UAE and Dubai.

The Arabic language currently ranks sixth among the languages of more than 6 billion people. There was, however, a time when Arabic was the lingua franca for science, mathematics, medicine, politics and diplomacy. Arab and Muslim scientists, mathematicians, architects, physicians and historians were the top teachers, philosophers and scientists for more than a millennium.

Modern civilization, however, encompasses much more. It is made up of trade, manufacturing, construction and hundreds of other activities. Yet, where in today's world can you find a mosque as beautiful and eternal as the Grand Mosque of Córdoba in Andalusia or a mausoleum as bright as the Taj Mahal in India?

In saying this, I am not trying to stir up old wounds intentionally or accidentally, and I would like to avoid both situations. Arabs respect other nations' civilizations and acknowledge their contribution to the human heritage. We also appreciate the pride other nations take in their respective civilizations, just like I am intensely proud of my own. The moment I hear the words 'Arab civilization', I know exactly what it means. I can cite scores of principles of our civilization, although there is one specific attribute that always captures my imagination, which summarizes everything in one word: 'pioneering', a word I will discuss later in the chapter.

When you face a challenge that demands a solution or a decision, you have two choices – you can either emulate the example set by others or use your own creativity and intelligence to formulate a new idea. This applied equally to the development of our country. Many brilliant ideas have circulated the globe and various nations have copied their concepts, so much so that these once inspired creations often become hackneyed. However, 'second-hand' ideas are not for us here in the UAE. We would far rather lead than follow.

At the root of any new project is an idea and if we cannot find a fresh concept for a project, we will not implement it because it will fall short of what we have come to expect. We believe that the shortest way to the bright future we seek lies in a creative and pioneering approach.

The credibility we now enjoy internationally has resulted in a number of other nations studying our solutions and adopting them. Although we are a small nation, we have enjoyed international exposure, and are managing and developing major projects in large and important countries such as India, South Korea and Hong Kong as well as in several Arab countries.

The large number of creative, highly qualified and motivated people who head and staff our team is ample proof that our empowerment policy is working. We will always strive to make this policy our top priority, based on our belief that our young UAE citizens are our most precious asset and the key to our future success. When I hear company managers complaining about a lack of qualified staff, I have to wonder how they have come to this conclusion when hundreds of well-trained, qualified UAE nationals, many of whom I have met both on official and non-official occasions, are available.

I believe the task of managers needs to include the selection of an appropriate number of suitably qualified UAE national staff, with an eye to succession. This does not apply only to companies, but in other areas as well, because it is a leader's duty to develop the leadership skills of those he believes are suitable. And when the time comes, these people can transfer their knowledge to the next generation.

While this happens most of the time, there are unfortunate exceptions. Some managers are not interested in – or will not tolerate – the existence of another person as qualified and skilled as they are, out of fear of competition or of losing their jobs. Although this is understandable to a degree, I disagree with such managers, because a true leader should realize he cannot be everywhere all the time and implement all his tasks at once. He must learn to delegate. When a leader fails to delegate, he will find himself embroiled in so much detail that it will eventually overwhelm him and distract him from his primary task (developing the business of the company and finding innovative solutions to its problems) to such an extent that he will eventually lose sight of the bigger picture.

But what exactly is the bigger picture?

The bigger picture is one of survival – life's driving force and the reason why all creatures spend each day trying to catch their prey or escape their hunters. Survival cannot be achieved by wishful thinking. Continued growth requires huge effort, complete attention and being consistently alert to potential dangers.

Although we live in a civilized society, the business world remains a jungle. Successful businessmen and women have learned to bide their time and wait for the right opportunities to present themselves. There is no room for error or sentiment, because it represents the difference between expansion and recession, fortune and bankruptcy, survival and death.

To illustrate this, during a Cabinet meeting to review our targets for e-government and e-commerce initiatives in the context of the latest developments worldwide, I explained the need for us to lead other nations in taking full advantage of the opportunities the new global economy has to offer. Some ministers did not believe this was necessary, saying we could deal with such matters once our economy was on a more solid footing.

My response was firm: "Where is the progress in keeping pace with the competition? If our sole goal is to attain the level others have reached, then we are setting our target too low. We must take matters into our own hands. Do not fool yourselves into believing that we are moving forward when we are only keeping up with general trends, while the real opportunities are slipping away."

We must take the lead and be proactive in forging our own destiny. The future will bring daunting, unforseen challenges and we must be ready to face anything.

God gave his believers sight, vision and perception, to understand their environment and the consequences of their actions, both today and tomorrow. God's glory is evident in everything. You see it in the contrast between people; you find it in the strong and the weak, the rich and the poor, the leader and the follower.

There was a time when Arabs were followers and their nations were subjugated. But when their luck changed, they became prominent nations that prospered in trade, architecture, science, arts and industry. Other nations looked to them and were inspired to follow their example.

The transformation occurred when Arab nations embraced the one word that summarizes the essence of our entire civilization: 'pioneer'. This concept filtered into every aspect of life – in peace, war, administration, science, architecture, trade, medicine, history, industry and diplomacy – becoming a philosophy that led the way. The revolutionary spirit continued unabated, not for two decades or five centuries, but for more than 1,000 years, and created a historic view of the Islamic Arab civilization as pioneers of excellence.

It is true, of course, that necessity is the mother of invention. Arabs put their pioneering spirit to work not for the acclaim they would receive in history, but out of a basic need to survive, progress and prosper.

Arabs embraced and developed several Roman administrative systems, including postage and currency, as a way to manage the affairs of the large populations and territory they had acquired. When Arabs invented the triangular-shaped lateen sail, they did so to allow their dhows to sail more efficiently, even in the absence of favourable winds. As a result, Arab merchants were able to seize the initiative and ship their goods to the ports of the Old World faster than ships with rectangular sails. In the process, they built substantial fortunes and created new job opportunities.

Scientific applications pioneered by Muslims are numerous. They excelled in geography, which was crucial for mapping borders along their trade routes, and in astronomy, which allowed merchants to sail at night using the stars and planets as their guides, instead of waiting until sunrise to resume their journeys. The development of the compass allowed Arab mariners to continue sailing at night even in cloudy weather and in high seas, instead of hugging coastal waters.

As a result of this ingenuity, Arab trade prospered, because merchants were able to quickly ship their goods between ports, including perishable cargo such as figs, which were exported from Malacca in Andalusia[3] to the Moorish[4] markets in the Maghrib[5] and to the Orient.[6] Arab merchants were present in all the ports of the Ancient World; they gained control of international sea lanes and their points of entrance and exit along a trade route that stretched for more than 10,000 kilometres from the north of China to Mombasa on Africa's east coast.

Some might wonder why the Arab nation did not just disappear in the thirteenth century, when the French and Spanish conquered Andalusia, rendering some two million people homeless, or when the Tartars conquered the Arab Orient in 1258 AD, totally destroying Baghdad and killing the Abbasid Caliph Al Musta'sim in the process. They survived because they still dominated the eastern sea trade routes, which, during that time, ensured their survival, even though other nations may have dominated on the battlefield.

These eastern trade routes remained under Arab control until the Portuguese navy conquered several major eastern sea trade ports in the sixteenth century. Arab fortunes and control of the trade dissipated and a new era of poverty and ignorance took root. Poverty, ignorance and a prolonged period of underdevelopment ensued, ending only a few decades ago.

Although the Portuguese were colonialists who dominated by sheer military power and devastation, their ships reached the Gulf, the Arabian Sea and India using Arab methods or tools modelled from Arab inventions, including navigational instruments such as the astrolabe, an instrument used before the development of the sextant, and the sextant itself. Hundreds of examples of these early inventions can be found in European and North American museums. Even the sea route to the Gulf and India was believed to have been revealed to the Portuguese by the famous Arab navigator, Ahmad Ibn Majid.[7]

The crucial point to remember here is that the pioneering Europeans forged ahead at the expense of the Arabs, who had lost their innovative spirit. The Portuguese became a revolutionary, seafaring and trading nation, and remained in power until the Moroccans killed their monarch, King Sebastian, in the battle of the Grand Castle (Al Qasr al-Kabeer) in 1578.

When nations lose their revolutionary spirit, attempts to regain it seem impossible. So even if the Portuguese had failed to completely crush Arab maritime trade, the Arabs would still have lost the trade war because their pioneering spirit had been quashed.

Although the triangular sail was decisive in its time and enabled the Portuguese and Spanish to reach and colonize the New World, it could not compete once steam and diesel-powered engines arrived on the scene. It became a symbol of the past.

When Arabs lost the trade war they began to lose other wars, along with their independence. They became imitators and followers. As Ibn Khaldoun said: "The vanquished are always fond of imitating the conqueror's mottos, attire, creed and other positions and customs."[8]

When great inventions began changing the face of the West, the Arab world was still living in the Middle Ages. The West emerged as the leader and grew in sophistication while subjugating entire nations, turning them into markets for their own products and purposes.

Arabs were pioneers once and we will become so once again. The twenty-first century brings with it a historical chance to transform our dreams into a concrete vision, provided we regain the core element we have lost – the pioneering spirit.

The new economy

Although some of us may prefer to turn a blind eye to the age of globalization, this is not an option; we have to embrace it wholeheartedly. We cannot ignore its effects because no matter what we do, it is here to stay. In order to bridge the huge gap between industrialized nations and ourselves, we must embrace the positive aspects of globalization, while evaluating and discarding the negative ones.

Globalization is the way forward; it is the environment in which international interaction will take place both now and in the future, and it is already taking root in the economy, productivity, communications and advanced technology. We have nothing to fear in the global race, because Islam's approach and message is universal; the Arab civilization is global in its essence and applications; and our vision for Dubai is all-encompassing in its concept, excellence and competitiveness.

Adopting a global stance in trade, economics, science and enlightenment brought Arabs and Muslims innumerable benefits and status in the past, and can do so once again under the umbrella of globalization. If we are enlightened and prepared to embrace globalization, we can enjoy our rightful share of the world's riches. Refuse it and we remain in the dark.

When we review the world's economic history, we see the distinct features of the two main productive ages it has experienced – the 'farming age' and the 'industrial age'. However, the last two decades have seen the emergence of a third economic age, dubbed by some as the 'information economy'.

This age consists of a closely-knit global economy that covers most fields and may therefore also be called the 'age of globalization'. Since this age requires extremely fast responses and depends on highly sophisticated technologies, it has also been called the 'age of technology'. It is, in fact, an invisible kind of economy that thrives on knowledge and creative ideas, and may therefore even be given a fourth name, the 'age of creative minds'. Let us hope they do not invent any more names to confuse matters further!

Whatever you call it, just as manufacturing did not replace farming, the information economy will not replace the industrial economy. As a matter of fact, the Industrial Revolution played a key role in developing agriculture, while new technologies have played a similar role in boosting industry.

The importance of the information economy is therefore not restricted to its intrinsic value as an independent sector, but encompasses its ability to energize agriculture, industry and services; as well as to boost their performance, reduce their costs, open new development horizons and create opportunities these economies cannot generate on their own.

If this is achieved, we will no longer be talking about a 'new' and an 'old' economy, but about a new 'information' economy and a 'traditional' economy. These complement each other, bringing in a new age of 'global' economy from which we ought to benefit. Embracing this will allow us to make up for the opportunities we lost during the commercial and industrial revolutions.

The new economy does not need huge manufacturing and production complexes, which means that the elements that secured the supremacy of industrialized nations are not the same ones that will provide nations with supremacy at this time. Today's giants might not be the same tomorrow, and those that are considered small today could well become the leaders of tomorrow.

Today's norms and considerations are no longer those that prevailed in the past, and the progress made possible by ultra-fast technologies will not take place in one or two phases at a time, but rather in leaps and bounds. The new economy ignores geographic and political boundaries, and opens its doors to all those who engage it. They will be able to work anywhere that the facilities and services essential to their businesses are available.

Who will pioneer the economy?

The pioneers will be those countries able to benefit from the opportunities presented by the new economy which, at the same time, will be ready to master the challenges, changes and problems generated by attempts to adapt to it – creative and agile countries that thrive on knowledge, information and ideas.

Dubai has the environment conducive to the success of businesses in the new economy. Among other factors, our expertise in international trade is widely acknowledged. We also boast some of the world's most sophisticated infrastructure, including modern office and residential complexes. Furthermore, we have already introduced the latest technologies into our economy, by creating the Middle East's first electronic free trade zone, accommodating Dubai Internet City and Dubai Media City, inaugurated in October 2000.

Despite all our achievements, if we want to lead in the new economy, we would still need to promote the quality of our services. I am committed to this goal and will ensure it is achieved. Another vision I wish to fulfil – and one that is no less important – is for Dubai to reach a pioneering status in all those businesses related to the new economy, not only locally and regionally, but globally as well. To assist in this objective, we will always strive to provide Dubai's business community with every advantage and amenity.

I fully understand the enormity of these ambitions and the changes needed to achieve them, but I am also aware of our huge potential. If we want Dubai to spearhead the new economy, we must change our concept of government and deal with the new economy in a different way. The introduction of e-government[9] in Dubai is just one of many necessary steps we need to take.

Governments are not the only parties affected by the new economy. In order to maintain success and excellence, trade, industry and services also need to respond to the crucial requirements of their economies and introduce any necessary changes.

Since we are a rich country, we should expect others to covet our wealth. Nations seldom enjoy total peace and stability. This never happened in the past and will not happen in the future.

If our thoughts focused only on war and the tensions surrounding us, our progress would grind to a halt. We do not want this to happen – we have already suffered greatly from being idle for so long. We must examine our problems meticulously and set the right course; one that will allow us to overcome any storm and reach safety before we can progress and achieve our goals.

People would tell me that there are risks in the new economy and I am aware of these risks. The Internet, for one, is neither good nor bad. We should take only what is useful and good and not accept anything that conflicts with our religion, customs and traditions. There were also those who complained that ambitious goals require so much effort. My response was always that I was aware of what is needed, but progress is an accumulative process. The West, for example, did not start the development of its transport infrastructure by constructing super highways; it first constructed simple, single-lane roads.

Others have pointed out the steps we need to take before we can avail of the opportunities offered by the new economy. I am also aware of these. One of the steps needed is to change our schools' curricula because they do not focus sufficiently on developing the creativity and skills of our students. Developing a more all-rounded education system is an immediate priority, to ensure that graduates will be suitably qualified for jobs in the future.

I believe some people face a situation where they are capable of speaking fluently about computers, software, the Internet, e-commerce and the new economy, but are unable to think along the lines of the new economy and understand its true demands. The most important of these requirements is to implement the idea immediately.

Some would argue that we can either hurry or slow things down, but I believe we have to start quickly and without making mistakes. Speed is necessary because the fastest overtakes the biggest.

We should always remember our competitors are trying just as hard as us to take the lead. In this age of technological revolution, when information travels at the speed of light, ideas can travel at the same speed. We must implement practical ideas without wasting any time. If we do not, others will – and they will also reap the rewards: wealth, large markets, job opportunities, stability, expertise, competitiveness and scores of other benefits. They will look forward to a bright future while the stragglers will remain in the dark.

We are living in an age where there is no room for hesitation. Many of the economic, technical and political concepts that prevailed during the last few years have been replaced by new concepts, ones that were imposed by necessity. Nations of all sizes are trying their best to adapt to the new realities and prepare their establishments, companies and citizens to face the challenges of the future. They are taking the measures needed to succeed.

This is a time when management concepts have changed. Some major multinationals have failed unexpectedly in the five years following 2001, while some small companies have prospered at an unprecedented pace. Major failures and fast growth usually do not happen gradually. The market value of companies worth billions can evaporate in a matter of days, while new technologies or products can add billions to the market values of small companies.

If superpowers realize they need to change their concepts, policies and laws in order to adapt to new realities, then why not us? If major multinationals, whose market values exceed the GDPs of a group of developing countries, realize the need to change their management concepts, why not our companies? And if universities, colleges and schools in industrialized countries are rapidly changing their curricula to meet the requirements of the new economy, what about our institutions of education?

Change and adapting to a quickly changing reality are inevitable. If we want to remain within the ranks of the advanced world, we need to match the speed at which the world is developing. We do not need the type of change that allows us to catch up or cope with others; we need the type that allows us not only to win the present race, but lead the next one. We have spent enough time in the shadow of our past and need to look forward and embrace our plans for the future.

Although this is a huge challenge, we enjoy crossing hurdles in the UAE. The existence of the UAE and its history are in themselves a challenge, while growth and continuity are some of the most important challenges facing GCC countries and the rest of the Arab world.

None of these are frightening when a leader is confident of himself and his people. On the contrary, challenges such as these promote resolve and determination, and generate creativity. I thus find myself eager to face every challenge head-on, without hesitation, and consider myself lucky to be living in an age so full of challenges.

Our world is new and totally different from the one our forefathers knew, but their world too was new compared to the one their ancestors knew. Just like us today, they had to wake up early and outpace others to survive and prosper. If they did not, we would not be here today. Each new generation faces new challenges and consecutive generations are, in a way, a succession of challenges.

Overcoming the challenges in the race for excellence is the secret of success; failing to do so is the reason behind defeat and trailing behind other nations.

The choice is ours.

---

1 Al Mansur or Abu Jafar Abdullah bin Mohammed Al Mansur (95–158 AH – 714–775 AD) was the second Abbasid Caliph (136–158 AH – 754–775 AD).

2 Al Tabari, Abu Jafar Mohammed bin Jarir (1985), *The History of Nations and Kings*, Beirut: Ezzeddine, vol. 4, p. 308.

3 The southernmost region of Spain, bordering on the Atlantic and the Mediterranean, with Seville as its capital, under Moorish rule at various times from 711 to 1492 AD.

4 The Moors are members of a northwestern African people of mixed Berber (indigenous people of North Africa) and Arab descent. They conquered the Iberian Peninsula in the eighth century and were driven out of their last stronghold in Granada at the end of the fifteenth century.

5 Also known as Maghreb, the region of Africa north of the Sahara and west of the Nile, coinciding with the Atlas Mountains. Its territories include Algeria, Libya, Morocco, Tunisia, Western Sahara and sometimes, Mauritania. Maghreb is almost entirely Muslim in religion.

6 Ibn Battouta, Mohammed bin Ibrahim Allawati (1980), *The Masterpiece of the Beholders about the Strangest Countries and Journeys: The Journeys of Ibn Battouta*, Beirut: Beirut Publishing House, p. 669.

7 Ahmad Ibn Majid (1421–1500) was an Arab navigator and cartographer born in Julphar, now known as Ra's al-Khaimah. He became famous in the West as the navigator who helped Vasco da Gama find his way from Africa to India.

8 Ibn Khaldoun, *The Muqaddimah of Ibn Khaldoun*, Beirut: Al Hilal, p. 101.

9 Dubai's e-government refers to Dubai Government's use of Information and Communication Technology to provide government services via an online portal to its citizens, residents and visitors, businesses and other government entities.

Part II

THE ELEMENTS OF THE DEVELOPMENT INDUSTRY

CHAPTER TWO

The Vision

Many years ago, some merchants came to me and asked me to approach my father, Sheikh Rashid, on their behalf, and discuss the large port he was planning at Jebel Ali.[1] Since the economy was in recession and we already had a large harbour at Port Rashid[2] that met their needs, they thought the emirate did not need a new, larger harbour.

I felt I should convey the message and shortly thereafter, went at dawn to the Jebel Ali area, where I knew I would find my father. He was standing on top of a small hill examining the site. I passed on the message and waited for his reply. He looked at me intently and said nothing, then he fumbled with the *midwakh*[3] he was holding between his fingers. After a few moments he looked at me again and then to the ground, saying nothing.

I dared not ask him the same question again, and waited until he had finished his examination and asked me to drive him home. Once we took off and after relaxing his feet against the corner of the door as usual, he said, "Listen my son, I never answered your question because I did not want the engineers to hear. But I can tell you that the reason I am building this port now is because there will come a time when you will not be able to afford to do so."

Before my father conceived and implemented this project, nobody had thought of executing one of such gigantic proportions. Even now, I have no simple explanation as to how the idea occurred to him, but if I had to explain it in one word, I would use the word 'vision'. In his great wisdom, God gave each one of us a share of material possessions, capabilities and talents. Some people may aspire to little more than their daily earnings, while others have far greater vision.

Just like mature trees, capabilities and feelings have deep roots. If we do not know the roots of things, or how to explain or define them, this does not mean they are rootless. An enlightened leader is capable of developing a vision and using his imagination to perfect it. It is like planting a tree and ensuring the branches grow upwards while the roots dig deep into the soil.

My father acquired leadership skills and the power of vision from my grandfather who, in turn, inherited his skills from his father. Such roots run very deep indeed. I am, after all, the son of an Arab tribe, and tribal people are schooled and groomed in wisdom and an acute awareness of future possibilities more by their parents than by schools.

Many great leaders never went to school, but gained their knowledge from the 'university of life' and by carefully observing everything that went on around them. Their teachers were the members of their tribes. This, of course, is why these leaders followed in the footsteps of their parents and why their education drew from their environment.

All the successive leaders of Dubai[4] enjoyed a clear and common vision of the emirate's future. My father's farsightedness was, however, ahead of its time simply because he was ahead of his time. Many officials in his entourage failed to understand his desire to implement all the mega projects he is now credited with and many also found it difficult to understand his ambitions.

He personally supervised trade and customs, looked after merchants' interests and solved their problems. He granted national and Indian merchants, and those from other nationalities, priority access to his majlis[5] even ahead of government officials. After the dawn prayers, he used to tour the city's projects one by one to make sure that work was going on as planned.

We have carried our father's flag just like he carried his father's flag, and we have continued his vision. The only difference is that he implemented his projects in the sixties and the seventies, while we are implementing similar ones in the twenty-first century. But we all still have the same goal of developing Dubai and securing the future comfort and security of its residents.

My father looked at the past with one eye and the future with the other. Similarly, we look at the achievements of my father with one eye and at our own plans with the other. Dubai International Financial Centre[6] is a clear example of a sustainable developement model that anticipated Dubai's immense growth. It opened Dubai to the world and attracted the world's attention to Dubai.

What else could this be but vision? If vision is not a science, what else is it? Is it an art? Talent? Does it evolve in an individual regardless of his environment or is it related to the latter? Is it inherited?

Whatever the case, vision should always incorporate one decisive element: it must allow for implementation. Conquering Constantinople was a vision for which Arabs raised huge armies and resources, and for which thousands died. But that great city refused to fall, reducing the Arab vision to nothing more than a dream.

On the other hand, conquering Constantinople was also a dream for the Ottomans until Mohammed the Conqueror[7] transformed it into a vision. Not only did he raise huge armies and resources, but he also adopted appropriate military tactics that allowed him to conquer the city.

Nevertheless, the feasibility of a vision is not enough. Visions do not make civilizations nor achieve growth and progress, unless the visionary in question transforms his vision into a reality within a reasonable period.

Many people talk about the 'Dubai Vision' when they ought to be talking about the 'vision for Dubai'. Vision was the start of what Dubai is today. This does not mean that we are at the end of the road because despite all our achievements, we are still at the beginning.

While vision is not a science, it is not an abstract idea either. It is a living extension of the visionary, pulsating with life just like him, growing and maturing with him, widening its horizons and deepening its experience along with him, jumping for joy when celebrating a success and feeling sadness with every failure.

History is not concerned with visions that are not implemented. My father made history because he implemented his vision and launched a huge drive in construction, building and trade, the like of which Dubai had never experienced before.

He taught me something that I also learned from Sheikh Zayed: to always strive to conquer the impossible. The first 'impossibility' we conquered was the establishment of the United Arab Emirates. When we think about this unique federation, we must recall the circumstances the country faced during that period.

The economy was weak, the planning limited, health care was basic and education was anything but widespread. There was foreign political pressure and scepticism about the chances of success. Some critics asked how a step like this could succeed "in an entity that does not have the necessary elements to constitute a state and at a time when all other federal attempts, between more sophisticated Arab countries have failed".

Sophistication had nothing to do with the failure of those attempts; they can only be attributed to the deficiencies of the Arab administrative systems of the time. The establishment of the UAE taught me about resolve and determination. It also taught me that there are leaders who care about the interests of their people.

This explains the success of a meeting held between Sheikh Zayed, in his capacity as the Ruler of Abu Dhabi, and my father, as the Ruler of Dubai, at the village of Al Samha, straddling the borders of both emirates. This meeting, held on 18 February 1968, resulted in an agreement of a federation between the two emirates, to become the nucleus of a larger one in the future. Indeed, by the end of 1971, a historical declaration established the UAE, activated the provisional constitution and declared Sheikh Zayed as the President of the new Federation.

The second 'impossibility' we overcame was the construction of Jebel Ali Port.[8] This project, which was realized within two years, was way ahead of its time when it was inaugurated in 1979. It was an undertaking of epic proportions for a small emirate such as Dubai and I doubt any consultant engineer would have wanted to undertake its feasibility study back then.

Imagine telling a group of investors: "This is the Jebel Ali area which, as you can see, is a remote area devoid of water, vegetation and people. I want to build the largest man-made port ever here, despite the fact that Dubai's Port Rashid is already the Middle East's largest port and has thirty-five berths."

I doubt that any of them would have been interested in investing hundreds of millions of US dollars in the project. They would have considered it impossible because the whole world was in a deep economic crisis at the time.

Two or three years before the economic slowdown, we used to see between 300 and 400 ships anchored off Dubai, queuing to offload their cargoes. Those ships disappeared when the economic crisis took hold of the region's economy. Most likely, the same investors would not have approved of my father's plan to "bring the sea to the port" using specially dredged lanes that would provide access for ships to the port.

Many people criticized my father's decision to build this port thirty-five kilometres south-east of Dubai for reasons which, at the time, must have seemed very sensible to them. Many also expected the project to fail, but my father had visualized the project in a manner that was nearly instinctive and went ahead with it. In doing so, he pushed the Emirate of Dubai forward and created a true monument from the sands of the desert.

I do not wish to endlessly stress the superb achievements of Sheikh Zayed and my father during the building of the Federation, because these achievements are evident everywhere in the UAE. I will simply say that they were the most astute people I have ever known; they overcame difficulties, achieved the impossible and transformed visions into realities. They ushered the UAE to its present status. It is no wonder that I share their ideals.

An original vision is one that allows you to grasp the future. A visionary leader should adhere to his vision, fully confident that he can see things that those in his entourage may not be able to perceive and that his vision will fulfil its set goals. Such a leader would also seriously consider any criticism of his vision and be prepared to defend it, convince others of its validity and efficiency, and overcome all obstacles obstructing its way.

The elements of a true leader's vision

A true leader's vision should target specific interests and answer important questions, such as:

1. What is the country's interest in this vision? What is the interest of its society and business community? Who will benefit from it and how? In what way will it promote development and enhance the achievements that have already resulted from previous visions?
2. Is the vision based upon specific plans or is it going to be implemented randomly, without any link between its different phases?
3. Is it realistic and feasible or is it a wild vision that no amount of financial and human resources are capable of realizing? For example, giant residential and tourist complexes such as The Palm[9] and The World[10] islands may require huge resources that many countries cannot afford. While they may be feasible in the UAE, it would be impossible to build them in a number of other places.
4. What is the ideal time to propose the vision?
5. What is the best way to implement it?
6. Is the executive team ready? Who are its members and where will we acquire the high-calibre skills necessary?
7. How will the implementation of the vision be financed?
8. How will we convince investors to finance the project?
9. How will we market the finished product and what is the target market? Where and when?

The features of a true leader's vision

1. The vision must be excellent in form, essence and implementation.
2. All its elements should include imagination.
3. It must be comprehensive and far-sighted.
4. It must be straightforward because clarity will make it easier to implement.
5. It must be challenging to some extent, not only for the project team, but for society as a whole.
6. Its announcement should have an impact.
7. It should stir the resolve, creativity and initiative in people and revive their determination to compete.

8. It should not be easy to implement and should border on the impossible without actually being so.
9. It should not be proposed prematurely, before perfecting it and linking all its various elements together.
10. It should benefit everybody in a comprehensive manner. The benefits should not be restricted to one or several groups of people.
11. It must be positive in that it promotes the people's trust in their leadership, their future and in each other. It must also deepen the people's trust in their country and their loyalty to it.

Implementing a true leadership vision

The operational plan: Vision can be seen as a gateway to a fully comprehensive operational plan, divided into several stages, each with its own designated implementation time. When I present my vision for a specific project, my message must be clearly understood by all those involved in its implementation. This is my vision, I want to implement it this way, within the set deadline; I want the project to operate this way; this is the number of companies involved, here is the work team, these are my sources of finance; and finally, this is what I expect the project to achieve.

The implementation phases: It is crucial to be aware of each and every stage of implementing the vision. The leader must know where he is going.

Mobilizing resources: The greatest challenge facing a leader is to be able to mobilize all those involved in implementing a vision and to guide them in achieving this common goal, as well as to mobilize all the efforts and resources needed to take it to a successful conclusion. My vision is not something I dream about while others make it a reality – I cannot sit in my office waiting for a miracle to happen. Implementing a vision requires an orderly, highly precise and committed common effort. Although common effort can be adopted for implementing a specific vision, it can also be applied in a much more comprehensive manner to more general visions.

For example, when I presented my vision for making Dubai the world's foremost financial and business centre in the first half of the twenty-first century, I asked all the government departments, organizations and officials involved in implementing this vision to cooperate and work hand in hand in their respective areas of speciality in order to transform it into reality. I also asked them the following:

- How many departments have a strategy for the future?
- Does each department have its own vision?
- How many departments have defined the elements for their success and set their own future goals?
- Did the people working in each department participate in this or were they at least introduced to the department's vision and mission?

Setting the framework of a project is one aspect; implementing it is another. So I told my team that after preparing a strategy for implementing the vision, defining the elements for its success and achieving its goals within the deadline I had set, I wanted to study it all, introduce any amendments I deemed necessary and complete the missing links before proceeding any further.

The work team: The shortest way to success in implementing a specific vision is to enlist the services of a talented, competitive and creative team, known for taking the initiative and acknowledged for their teamwork.

Timing: Preparing fully comprehensive plans does not mean a thing unless these plans are implemented strictly on schedule. The leader must set a time limit, not only for the implementation of each vision, but also for each of their stages. My vision is not an open-ended undertaking and I am not the only one with a vision in this world. Many people have visions bigger than mine and have more financial clout than me. This tells me that I must implement mine before them or lose the opportunity to realize it – a belief which has helped me achieve success in many of endeavours. Timing is also crucial for the later stage of marketing, which explains the need to adhere to the set delivery dates under all circumstances.

The development industry

Can we race a horse without a jockey?

Vision is a race for victory in a bloodless battle for development. Development today is not a trend, but a full-blown industry. And since it is an industry, it must generate products that have certain elements. The first of these is vision. A good leader crystallizes his vision, defines its objectives, navigates its development and supervises its implementation. Failure in defining the objectives and following the implementation is a true recipe for disappointment.

Even when running the world's best horse, we cannot expect to win a race if we do not have the right jockey. Similarly, having a vision and setting its targets and the elements for its success are essential for a country to improve its performance, services and the efficiency of its response to future developments. This should be done with one goal in mind: that of serving the people and enhancing the status of the country. This is what I expect our development industry to deliver.

I do not see progress as a wish or a favour, or even a gesture of generosity on the part of the leader, but as a permanent, unconditional commitment by the leader, the government and all civil servants, towards the nation. This requires all of them to strive to develop the country, within the framework of a clearly defined development strategy that must be carried out to the letter.

If development is the government's top priority, it is the duty of the country's citizens and in many cases, its resident expatriates, to contribute to the success of the process. But this can be achieved only if every citizen and resident expatriate feels he or she is part of the ongoing development process and has a stake in its success.

Dubai hosts expatriates of all nationalities. The homelands of some of these people have failed to make peace with their neighbours and might be witnessing tension that borders on war from time to time. The UAE is dedicated towards bringing peace to all the nations of the world. We believe that war very rarely settles a problem that peace cannot solve, and that calm dialogue is more effective than tension and implacability.

The UAE, however, chooses not to expend its energies in tension, wars or disputes. Dubai's residents primarily focus their energies on collectively enhancing their quality of life, contributing to the emirate's prosperity and building its present and future. Perhaps Dubai is not the place for anyone who believes otherwise. I believe all the people living and working in Dubai are aware of these facts, abide by them and know their limits, responsibilities and duties. Dubai is a city of peace and civilization; a place for work, production and pioneering ideas.

Dubai is recognized as one of the safest cities in the world. This is true; we have a high level of security and a capable, modern police force. But this is not the main reason for the level of security and peace of mind we enjoy. The people of Dubai are the true policemen and protectors of the law and because they have invested their interests and futures in Dubai, they all guard it and protect it just as if they were defending their own interests and families.

Expatriate residents live in peace and harmony in Dubai as friends, neighbours and colleagues, because they know that this is essential for protecting their welfare, regardless of the tensions between their countries.

Dubai needs the efforts, creativity and contribution of all its residents. Whoever has a stake in Dubai's present will have a stake in its future, provided he or she works toward this goal. If they do not, Dubai is not the right place for them.

Anyone living in Dubai and not enjoying a good standard of living must understand that there is something wrong and they must address and correct this mistake. While it is possible that the fruits of Dubai's development may not yet have reached everybody, Dubai is not the place for people who are strong and healthy, but have no contribution to make, or are simply not prepared to work hard for success.

There are always those who need help in every community – and these people will receive help in Dubai – but the rest must wake up early, race, trade, manufacture, produce, build and make profits, in an atmosphere of positive competition, security and hope, because this is what Dubai is about.

I believe promoting this kind of environment should top the priorities of any developmental vision and that providing the conditions leading to such an environment should be the ultimate priority of all the world's governments. It is not enough that a government provides these facilities for the present; it must ensure it provides them tomorrow, next year, in the next decade and in the future.

Furthermore, it is not enough for the governments to develop traditional economies. They must lay the foundations for the new economy, by developing the necessary legal, economic and technical structures.

And, finally, it is not enough for governments to simply look towards the future but to actually live it by trying to anticipate all the challenges of tomorrow and preparing the right plans to face them.

As I already mentioned, the younger generation is the future of this country. They are the ones who will find the formula that will guarantee sustainable development process and stability both for themselves and for future generations.

The success of our younger generation is not a success for the UAE alone, but a success for Arabs everywhere. They are the prime target of any economic vision and every development effort. Any development vision must therefore aim at preparing the younger generation not only to keep pace with the new economy, but to also take the initiative and lead.

This requires change – a change in the curriculum, training and thinking, as well as in government procedures and priorities. Like the new economy itself, most of the tools are new and the necessary changes should be introduced to allow them to be used successfully.

Success in business and ventures has its acknowledged elements, but nothing is more important than specialization in the age of specialization, professionalism in the age of professionalism and technology in the age of technology. Our age is one of great ideas and innovation that produce outstanding projects, and not one of filling minds with information. A hundred successful projects can provide job opportunities for tens of thousands of people and make the world a better place for future generations.

Our younger generation must not only be taught the whole spectrum of available knowledge, they must acquire and master practical skills and competencies by working in companies and on projects as a first step towards establishing their own successful ventures. They should also be given the chance to interact with the business community and market, enabling them to develop and enrich our national economy.

We should not settle with providing our youth with the best schools, colleges and universities. We must also provide them with specialized institutions capable of promoting their initiative and innovative spirit. We must help them develop their business and entrepreneurial skills. We must contribute towards transforming their bright ideas into successful ventures and provide the advice, investment, management and marketing resources needed to bring these ventures to fruition.

Although businessmen and women have to shoulder major responsibilities in achieving this, government officials must bear the heavier responsibility of coaching the younger generation and guiding them in the right direction. Young people cannot shape a future befitting them, their nation and their country, without being provided with incentives, coaching, love and care.

Nations are only as successful as their younger generations, and achieving success is a national responsibility, not limited to governments only. The government will stand for its responsibilities, yet the private sector plays a fundamental role in supporting the sons and daughters of the UAE, the comprehensive leap in development and the nation's prosperity.

This is our way to the future and the general direction of our development vision. Development is an accumulative process and shaping the future is an endless one. Sheikh Zayed and my father paved the road to development, progress and creativity, and it is up to us to continue in the same direction. Development is a tough process full of successes and pitfalls. This applies to all the civil servants employed by the Government of Dubai and most of all, to me. We have achieved much but are only at the beginning of the road. Let us join hands, look to the future and push ahead on the road to excellence.

---

1 Jebel Ali is a port town, located 35 kilometres southwest of the city of Dubai
2 Port Rashid, also referred to as Mina Rashid, is a man-made commercial port in Dubai. Named after Sheikh Rashid bin Saeed Al Maktoum, the port opened in 1972.
3 A small Arabic pipe manufactured locally from wood.
4 Historians point to 1833 as the start of Dubai's modern history. In that year, some 800 members of the Al Bu Falasah branch of the Bani Yas tribe seceded from Abu Dhabi and migrated to Dubai, where they settled along the banks of the Creek. They were led by Maktoum bin Buti Al Maktoum and Ubaid bin Saeed until the death of the latter in 1836, leaving Sheikh Maktoum in sole power. This was the start of the Maktoum dynasty that lasts to this day.
5 Arabic for 'assembly'. Also used to describe the place where a ruler regularly meets his courtiers, retinue, and other visitors or guests.
6 Dubai International Financial Centre (DIFC) is an onshore financial hub, strategically located between the east and west. It creates an environment for growth, progress and economic development in Dubai and the wider region by providing the necessary legal, business and physical infrastructure, benchmarked against international standards.
7 Mohammed the Conqueror, also known as Sultan Mehmed II (30 March 1432–3 May 1481) was the Sultan of the Ottoman Empire for a short time from 1444 to 1446, and later from 1451 to 1481.
8 Jebel Ali Port is a deep port located in Jebel Ali, Dubai. Jebel Ali Port is the world's largest man-made harbour and the biggest port in the Middle East. It was constructed in the late 1970s to supplement the facilities at Port Rashid.
9 The Palm Islands are an artificial archipelago in Dubai. Major commercial and residential infrastructures were constructed by Nakheel Properties, a company owned by the Dubai government. The islands are the Palm Jumeirah, the Palm Jebel Ali and the Palm Deira.
10 The World or World Islands is an artificial archipelago of various small islands constructed in the rough shape of a world map, located 4 kilometres off the coast of Dubai. The World islands are composed mainly of sand dredged from Dubai's shallow coastal waters, and are one of several artificial island developments in Dubai.

CHAPTER THREE

Leadership

I once asked various government department heads to organize a series of lectures and seminars to discuss topics in their respective domains and competencies. Among other things, these were to focus on specific issues, such as community services and upgrading human resources and creative skills.

Since the proposed meetings aimed to shed light on the problems facing our development process, determine its targets and benefit from our mutual experience, it was suggested that I deliver the opening address and focus on leadership. Given that leadership is in my blood, I accepted, thinking that it would not be difficult at all.

But as the date drew nearer and I started planning my address, I soon realized that while assuming leadership is one thing, explaining it is something completely different. Although I can talk about the various departments of the Government of Dubai with authority and assume the role of a leader every hour of my life, I found it to be a challenging subject.

Of course, we all know what 'leader' and 'leadership' mean, but what we tend to forget is that there are different types of leaders and leaderships. The leader of a select group of people is not the same as one leading an army or a country. While most people are well equipped to lead in a limited domain, leading countries and nations requires a lot more. Some may say leaders are born and not made, which may or may not be true. Others say that leadership cannot be learned, because it is something you either have or do not.

Based on experience and observation, we can say with reasonable confidence that leadership is a gift that some people have and others do not. Even if we managed, theoretically, to determine all the qualifications necessary to make a leader and implant them in a certain person, doing this would not necessarily produce a leader. Implanting a single human trait in an individual can be a very difficult undertaking; imagine how ambitious it would be to implant a whole set of sophisticated and complex traits in that same person. Surely this would be an almost impossible task, given the different biological, social and political circumstances we face?

We can conclude from this that there is no mould in which we can put human traits and produce a leader, and also that there are no common factors between leaders. Not everyone born on a Friday, at the beginning of the month, or who has graduated from Sandhurst, West Point, Oxford, Harvard – or some other famous military academy or university – is fit to become a leader. That is why I have said that leadership is one of the most complicated issues to explain.

I believe that one of the reasons for this lies in the talents, feelings and powers a leader possesses. Such features cannot be easily measured or defined, which explains why some people describe them with words such as 'magical' or 'astute'. Personally, I prefer to talk about 'leadership spirit'. Leadership spirit cannot be implanted or removed, because it is deeply rooted in genealogy, upbringing and instinct, while its branches are perfected by several factors such as time, wisdom, science, expertise, experience, dexterity and contact with others, assimilating their skills.

Leadership and excellence

History has shown us that there are different types of leaders, most of whom were propelled to notoriety by events and circumstances and were thus categorized by history as leaders. An even rarer type of leader is one who uses his astuteness, intelligence and leadership skills to produce events that shape life and consequently, history. The most gifted leader is, however, one who does not shape only the present, but a good part of the future as well.

Although Arab and world history abound with numerous examples of such leaders, if I were to review the history that I stood witness to, the leader I constantly think about is Sheikh Zayed. My relationship with Sheikh Zayed was so full of love and sincerity, that it was one of father and son. Sheikh Zayed earned the love of all those around him, out of their great respect for his hard work and achievements. He was also frank and expected people to be frank with him. This is something he taught me and this is how I came to respect him.

I have already explained how Sheikh Zayed showed me the way towards conquering the impossible and I can now add that he also taught me the true meaning of love. No one who ever met Sheikh Zayed could help but love him for his transparency, genuine Arab spirit, simplicity, good faith and his frank political stance. When he talked, he never tried to please anyone, but sought only to please God and his conscience.

He was a man who had faith in God, his country, his people and himself; a man of his word, who always kept his promise and helped his neighbours. These are the qualities of a great leader, but another is a rare gift from God – to be blessed with the love of his people. A leader might be feared or respected, but to be truly loved by his people is something every leader aspires to achieve.

Sheikh Zayed also taught us that leadership is all about daily action and not just theory. Leadership, as he practised it, is a human and social concept that overtakes speculation. It is also about determination, self-confidence, far-sightedness and good judgement.

When all or most people concerned approve of an idea you have proposed and have successfully implemented, no one will deny that you have achieved something worthwhile. But in my opinion, true excellence is when you propose an idea that may be good, but does not necessarily gain everybody's immediate approval, and you have to overcome obstacles to implement it.

This cannot be accomplished through ordinary vision, but requires a leader who is ahead of his time and looks to the future; one who does not only dream, but has a true vision and follows the right development path – a leader who will lead his people to a better future.

How can I prove this? Well many people, from the United Arab Emirates and overseas, criticized Sheikh Zayed for drilling artesian wells in the desert and using the water for farming. They said this would deplete a nonrenewable resource, inflict heavy damage on the environment and disturb its natural balance. Although none of those critics ever knew the actual size of the underground water reservoirs, they continually criticized the idea.

As time passed, water remained abundant and none of the fears of critics materialized, while Sheikh Zayed was proven right. In the not-so-distant past, people travelling between Abu Dhabi[1] and Al Ain[2] would die of thirst if they did not have enough water for the long journey. Sheikh Zayed transformed the same journey into a fascinating drive on an ultramodern highway flanked by farms, palm gardens and endless greenery.

In fact, Sheikh Zayed transformed a large area of the Emirate of Abu Dhabi into the world's largest oasis in one of the world's harshest deserts. All this was made possible by the huge water reserves he put to good use and which are now expected to last many decades.

The second example of the value of true visionary leadership comes from my late father, Sheikh Rashid. He also chose one of the world's harshest deserts – and one of Dubai's remotest and most isolated areas – to invest hundreds of millions of US dollars in building the world's largest man-made port and the Gulf's largest free trade and industrial zones.

Although the projects were widely criticized all around the world, my father proved that he knew what he was doing and had correctly identified the huge benefits this rare opportunity had to offer in the future. He grasped the opportunity and succeeded in his endeavour.

What else did he prove?

He proved that a great leader should avail himself of brilliant opportunities whenever he can – and if he is not able to find such opportunities, he should make them.

Leadership qualities

A leader may be able to foresee something no one else can. This is one of the qualities that make true leaders. They must always look forward, further than anyone else, in order to anticipate the future, predict the challenges it will bring, and prepare their people to face them. We cannot sit idly by and say that we do not know what will happen in the future, because if we let events shape our future, they could dictate a scenario that we do not want; and if we let others make our future, they will give us the future they want and not one that we envisage.

If we do not choose the future, we will be choosing the past. Our past was glorious, but it cannot dictate our present or our future. We are not required to free ourselves from our past, because it lives in our conscience, but we have to free ourselves from staying in the past. Our present should be our starting point and the future should be our target. We must decide how to build the future.

When leaders have the ability to foresee the future – as well as the road leading to it – they are the best people to fulfil its promise. However, if we fail for any reason, we must relinquish leadership to others more capable of realizing the vision. We must plan, endeavour, innovate and do our best to reach our goals, and then let God do the rest.

I consider the officials of the Government of Dubai as the leaders of our people because of their substantial responsibilities and their senior positions in the government. While I can provide advice, guidance and encouragement to help us achieve our mutual goals, I cannot make each and every one of them a leader on my own.

Together, we can establish the qualities of a leader at all levels, right to the top of the pyramid. All officials can determine whether they have the qualities that make a leader. If they conclude they do not have what it takes, they might decide to improve their performance, acquire new skills and explore their hidden potential, so that they can discharge their duties as best they can.

The qualities leaders at all levels should possess include the following (for the sake of simplicity, I have used the male gender in this list and elsewhere, but hasten to add that any leader could just as easily be female as male):

1. The ability to lead from the front, to take the initiative and tell those following him, "This is our target, so follow me to it," instead of saying, "I am right behind you."

2. To give his people's interests top priority, embody their aspirations, meet their needs and formulate equations that can achieve these goals, through one or more visions with specific objectives and implementation stages.
3. To adopt decisions which fulfil the aims of his vision, and to be ready to battle the odds, even though not all members of his team might agree with him.
4. To shoulder his responsibilities and discharge them as best he can. True leaders should take the blame for wrong decisions. They should be prepared to say, "I am the leader and I am the one who made these mistakes," and on the other hand, credit success to his team. A true leader does not evade the consequences, no matter how harsh they might be. He actually enjoys bearing responsibility and even looks for it.
5. To meet any crisis head-on, face the difficulties preventing him from reaching his targets and remove any obstacles impeding the way to success. A leader must meet the expectations of his team and always set an example for his followers. This does not mean that he should be involved in solving all the problems, big and small, as he should always respect the chain of command, while all members of the team should understand and follow this chain.
6. To empower others, which is easier said than done, because, after all, we are all human and many people tend to be egoistical and lack the power and humility of a true leader, giving themselves precedence over everybody else.
7. To consult with others and engage in dialogue. God urged faithful Muslims to consult one another and said in the Holy Qur'an, "And consult with them upon the conduct of affairs."[3] Our Prophet Mohammed (PBUH) was our example for the importance of consultation. Abu Hurairah,[4] one of the most learned companions of the Prophet (PBUH), said, "I have not seen anyone who consulted with his companions more than Mohammed the messenger." Good

advice can correct a wrong step taken and other mistakes. Some leaders turn their noses up at consultation and consider it a sign of weakness, but I believe it promotes the leader's power and the respect of his followers. When Sheikh Zayed asked for my opinion about a certain issue, I used to wonder what I could possibly say, when I was certain he already knew much more about the issue and its solution than I did. Leaders always try to gain knowledge from their acquaintances, because no one really knows where the next bright idea or suggestion may come from. They are perceptive and realize that they cannot judge people solely by their appearance and position. Consultation has other benefits too, such as being a sure way to promote better knowledge and decisions. It can also broaden your horizons and assist leaders in their decisions. If those consulted provide advice in good faith and are sincere, courageous and frank, then consultation can be a process of accountability. This does not weaken a leader's position but on the contrary, strengthens it, because his final goal is to serve public interest and not personal ones.

8. A leader should set clear goals for himself and his team so that he can interact with them and unequivocally commit himself to his goals. If he lost this commitment and interaction, he would lose his ability to see clearly and both he and his followers could lose track of the right course.
9. A leader draws his power from his faith in God, his country and his determination – not from the strength of his guards and escort.
10. A leader is self-confident by nature. If he was not, he would not be able to trust anyone. A true leader must therefore trust his team, his country and his people, and link this trust to his determination to implement his vision and plans under all circumstances.
11. Knowledge is essential in making the right decisions. A leader must know how to execute his job and have the mental and physical qualifications that enable him to carry out his duties. A leader does not follow working hours and has no weekends or holidays. He must

always be alert and ready to take the necessary decisions anytime, day or night. We cannot expect leaders to be impeccable orators and writers, but they must be fluent enough to express themselves clearly. Our drill sergeants at the military academy insist on mastering this skill all the time. A leader must know how to deliver his instructions to his team in a way that guarantees they clearly understand them before implementing them, leaving no chance for misunderstanding and errors. The use of complex ideas, vague images and difficult-to-understand language using 'big' words is a waste of time and raises more questions than answers. Some of those who hear these types of instructions do not actually listen to them, while others may interpret them incorrectly. This leaves ample space for different interpretations and courses of action. A leader must use simple, everyday speech, explain himself clearly without too much detail, and avoid detours and repetition.

12. A leader should also clearly define the message he wants to convey and carefully select the words he uses with his audience. Since speech is not the only means of communication between people, a leader must always monitor the reaction and behaviour of his audience. He must choose the right words for the right occasion and deliver well-articulated ideas in a clear voice, using harmonious gestures and a presentation technique representative of the leadership's status and prominence, in order to promote confidence in his subordinates and his image among them. Stuttering, hesitation, mediocre performances and too much repetition do not reflect a good leader.
13. It is the duty of any leader to persuade his people to accept his visions and goals, in order to enlist their full cooperation in implementing them. In addition, he must always be ready to defend his decisions and vision, using his power of persuasion, sound reasoning and accurate data.
14. Although the allegiance of subordinates to their leader is important, his devotion to them is even more crucial. The same goes for trust

and respect. These are interconnected relationships and links of the same chain; the moment one of them breaks, for whatever reason, confidence will break down and will be extremely difficult to restore. It is therefore very important that no party to this kind of relationship pushes the other party into losing his/their confidence.

15. It almost goes without saying that when a leader motivates and encourages the members of his team, they will enjoy their work and be inspired to greater achievements.
16. A leader should be the symbol of a society and a living example to the younger generation. A successful leader must set a good example for his team – how can he expect their commitment if he himself is not completely committed? How does a leader expect his team to earn the respect of the public and provide it with good services if he himself does not respect them, solve their problems or interact with them sufficiently? An Arab proverb says, "be their example and you will secure their proficiency." A leader therefore needs to set the example through his humbleness, personal character, shouldering of responsibilities, fairness and objectivity.

The visible and invisible aspects of leadership

Some team members are highly knowledgeable in their domains of expertise, hence it is imperative for a leader to always seek the advice of experts and well-informed people, and assimilate their opinions to reach the right decisions. Anybody may provide suggestions, but the leader alone must have the final say, because he is the one who carries the responsibility. That is why we always adopt the formula, 'many minds, one opinion'.

Sometimes, an unforeseen event may obstruct the implementation of an idea that was conceived and planned by a leader. In such a case, the leader should utilize his crisis management skills – he should study the reasons, determine the best form of corrective action and instruct relevant officials to take the necessary precautions, in order to prevent such an interruption from recurring.

The opposite can also happen, such as when unforeseen catalysts expedite the progress of a project, making it happen more quickly and with greater benefits than originally planned. A good example of this is Emirates Airline, which started with just two chartered jets in 1985 and quickly grew into a full-fledged international airline, with a fleet projected to number some 150 jet aircraft by 2012.[5]

Is it luck or something else? Some people attribute success to the luck of the leader, but the luckiest leader is the one who makes his own luck.

Opportunities are made, they do not just lie around waiting for someone to grab them. A true leader must make his own opportunities and always be ready to use them as quickly as possible. True and original leadership must be free of arrogance, condescension, overconfidence and the belief that one is incapable of ever being wrong. The Prophet Mohammed (PBUH) once said, "No one with the slightest particle of faith in his heart will enter hell and no one with the slightest particle of arrogance in his heart will enter heaven."[6]

A leader must know that implementing one or two successful projects does not give him the right to feel superior to others and to start boasting. These are the symptoms that drive a leader to believe he is infallible. Once a leader reaches that point, he starts regressing and drives himself and his nation into a bottomless pit.

Observe where leaders of this type in the Arab world and elsewhere drove their people. Regardless of their countries, all dictators are like this, just as if they all graduated from the same school. New dictators, however, do not seem to have studied their history, and ignore the fact that all dictators fail in the end and draw their countries with them into failure, destroying not only their own achievements, but also those of their predecessors in the process.

We are at the beginning of the road and therefore have no reason to feel arrogant. Although leaders alone bear the responsibility of falling victims to this, sycophants can pave the way for some leaders to fall into this trap. A leader must surround himself with people who provide him with good and sincere advice, not people who advise him one day and deceive him the next. A true leader must reject sycophancy, because he does not need anyone to tell him he is a leader. He already knows what he is.

Anyone who admires his leader greatly, and seeks his respect and trust, should be frank with him, tell him about his mistakes and faults, and advise him about the right way. In addition to avoiding sycophants and trivia, a leader should also focus on self-discipline, managing his behaviour and adopting good policies. He also needs to realize the importance of his position, understand the limits of his power, the capabilities of his people and nation, and dedicate his time, efforts and intellect to serving his people.

There are, of course, various kinds of leaders and the differences between their capabilities and competencies can sometimes be difficult to comprehend. Perhaps some capabilities and competencies are tangible, but leadership is not.

I previously talked about 'leadership spirit' and I would now like to expand on that. A leader might sometimes feel that he has adopted the right decision, 'led by his heart' according to a popular saying, but this belief might also be clouded by some apprehension. He might say, "Something inside me drove me to adopt this approach and reject the other." This means that a leader has leadership instincts, which he may sometimes be unable to explain.

But how does a leader do this and from where does he derive such powers? Do they result of an accumulation of knowledge, life experience and political, social and economic data? Or do they take root in his subconscious mind? Are they something in his genes? How does he know which is the right decision and which is the wrong one? Is it an innate power that encompasses all the previous factors in addition to others, about which we know nothing? And how can we possess such powers?

To summarize, I might say that every leader is endowed with scores of characteristics, qualities and powers in his conscious and subconscious mind, and their surrounding realms. Excellent leadership is the natural product of constant creativity, hard work and the power to motivate others. This is not the final word because leadership is an ongoing process.

I said at the beginning of this chapter that I consider leadership one of the most difficult concepts to explain and I have no choice but to repeat this at the end.

---

1 Abu Dhabi is the capital and the second largest city of the United Arab Emirates in terms of population, and the largest of the seven member emirates of the UAE.
2 Al Ain, also known as the Garden City owing to its greenery, is the second largest city in the Emirate of Abu Dhabi and the fourth largest city in the UAE.
3 *Sahih Muslim*, narrated by Muslim Ibn Al Hajjaj Al Nisaburi and freely translated from the Arabic.
4 Abd Al Rahman Ibn Sakhr Al Azdi (603–681) was a companion of the Prophet Mohammed (PBUH) and the narrator of the hadith most quoted in the *isnad* (chain of transmission) by Sunnis.
5 Emirates Airline now operates over 180 jet aircraft.
6 Sura Al Omran, v. 159.

CHAPTER FOUR

Management

Someone once suggested that because of the difficult circumstances facing the Arab world and the constant aggression against Palestine, I should postpone a meeting relating to the Dubai Government Excellence Programme[1]. I told him that despite his sentiments and patriotic feelings, these very events made that meeting imperative. He looked astonished and asked me why it was that important. I started to explain, wondering how he failed to understand that management was one of the major factors in addressing the situation the Arab world is presently witnessing.

The Prophet Mohammed (PBUH) was reported to have said, "Abu Hurairah, do you want me to show you the way to one of paradise's treasures? They say there is no power but that of God, and there is no escape from God but to God."[2]

Ever since I began to understand the world around me, I have never seen a time when the Arab nation has not faced critical difficulties, or has not been under constant aggression or at war. I therefore believe that "there is no power but that of God." The remedy for all our problems lies in consolidating our ranks, rejecting bilateral feuds and surmounting the petty differences that divide us, instead of deepening them further.

One day, conflicts will end and Arabs will regain their rights everywhere. Jerusalem will revert to its rightful owners. With the siege lifted, all Arabs will be able to enjoy independence and freedom, and focus all their efforts on regaining their pioneering status.

The crisis the Arab world is facing today is not one of money, men, morale, land or resources – it is a crisis of management.

If Arab management systems were efficient, Arab politics, economy, education, media, government services, culture, arts and everything else would excel. But if the performance and concepts of management in all fields and at all levels are not upgraded, we will be left standing. Ignoring shortfalls in management is the quickest way for underdevelopment to continue unchecked. Despite this awareness, I do not see any concerted Arab effort to resolve this situation.

Good management requires a capable manager. The Arab world has politicians aplenty, more than it really needs, but we lack creative managers who can lead us out of the constant crises we are facing. Our need for lengthy speeches, statements and eloquent words is far less important than our need for people who can build airports, ports, companies, factories and other growth-generating ventures. These all require managerial skills capable of mobilizing the resources needed to reach specific targets within a defined time frame.

Management is more than just a word; it is a full-fledged science. Management might require different remedies for each problem, but in essence, the same applies to politics, the economy, sports and every other sort of human activity. The final goal of management is to choose the best policies and decisions from the options available, and convert them into targets for which results can be measured precisely.

The whole managerial exercise should focus on reaching targets and serving those who are meant to be served. Unless this happens, management will not even be able to direct itself, let alone their departments, and we will suffer from bureaucracy, lost opportunities and a waste of resources.

Part of our problem in the Arab world is that many decisions do not serve the real interests of Arabs, nor improve their economic and living conditions, but are meant rather to please them. This is not the cure our community needs but a drug that partially dulls the pain, only to see it recur with added venom.

Our leaders in the United Arab Emirates have taught us to work for the common good of the country and its citizens. The relationship between the leadership and the people is similar to that between parents and children. Children, as most parents know (and I am one of them), often dislike orders and instructions. Some of them detest studying and others do not even want to go to school, preferring to be left to do whatever they like. And of course, allowing such behaviour does not make a good parent.

If parents are serious about their children's future, they should be equally serious about how they deal with them. They should urge them to study at the right time; teach them to respect themselves, their family and others; and help them develop the best behaviour at home, at school and elsewhere. If parents want to help their children successfully move from one stage of life to another, they need to exercise the appropriate amount of firmness.

Although this might be a bitter pill for some, it is not a high price for securing a healthy mind for each and every one of our children. And who does not want health and wealth for their children or their community?

Sometimes, moving on from studying to working does not change the situation much. Some people live a monotonous life and prefer monotonous work; others are reluctant by nature and happy to work slowly. Then, there are also those who have no wish to burden their minds and choose only the easiest tasks, leaving the more important ones for their colleagues.

People act this way in company offices, government departments and other places of work because they grew up accustomed to these ways at home and at school. Management train their staff, provide them with skills, broaden their career horizons and sometimes even teach them good behaviour, but the workplace is not a substitute for home or school – it is a place for production.

An employer needs to manage his business and should not have to waste precious time dealing with laxness in employees. Addressing irregularities at this late stage can be a lot worse than the bitter pill that should have been taken earlier and may result in penalties, suspension of promotion and worse still, dismissal. What can we do with such people? How can we convince them that work is an essential part of life and that they are being paid a salary to work in a specific capacity, and not to fritter away time during working hours?

Most people are capable of working hard and everyone can do more than they are actually doing. We must therefore revert to the parent–

child example, and adopt methods that put an end to their complacency and professional weaknesses, thereby pushing them back to work, productiveness and success.

Routine is the enemy of the pioneering spirit. We need to avoid routine practices and adopt a creative frame of mind to achieve success. Anyone interested in joining the race must commit to it fully. Laziness only leads to more laziness, while work ensures joy and the path to success.

We should not be afraid of hard work, challenges and pressure because they will come our way no matter what, and will make us better people. A diamond is nothing more than a stone until it is cut and polished; only then does it become a precious stone. But what is it that polishes a manager? Work experience and commitment.

Since we have not reached our destination, we cannot rest on our achievements. When we reach that destination, we will probably find that it is only an interim goal and that we will need to keep running. If we take a break, we will find others beating us to the winning post. If your drive and ambition disappear for whatever reason, reawakening it would be a very difficult task. The Arab world is testimony to this.

We can provide scores of excuses to justify our managerial backwardness; we can blame circumstances or other people, and we can complain about the lack of suitable conditions and so on. But in the end, we only have ourselves to blame. When we fail to manage our development, economy, investment and human resources, it is only normal that we fail in everything else.

In the early sixties, South Korea was poorer than Egypt and facing military and economic pressures similar to those we are witnessing in the Arab world today. These circumstances did not, however, deter that country from becoming a major industrial power. Similarly, Taiwan and many other countries managed to evolve from basic economies into industrial powerhouses within the span of a few decades, and against the backdrop of very difficult political and economic circumstances. It is no longer possible or correct, therefore, to use major national issues as an excuse for our managerial failures.

Our experience in the UAE has taught us that the difference between good and bad government sometimes lies in the number of obstacles we can remove from the path of our citizens or put before them. Most of the Arab world suffers from self-imposed obstacles – those facing students, businessmen, traders, investors, creative people and women.

Most of the Arab world also suffers from bottlenecks. These are evident in airports, in processing formalities and in other areas. You would be forgiven for thinking Arab governments are not interested in relieving bottlenecks in order to promote business and talent, and allocate the remaining time to work, production and the generation of wealth.

You would also be forgiven for thinking these governments are closing every door that allows efficiency to penetrate. Why is the relationship between the citizen and the civil servant so distorted?

Is the citizen supposed to be at the service of the civil servant or the civil servant at the service of the citizen?

We Arabs can give much more of ourselves than we are currently giving. We can be much more creative. We can race and win. In Dubai, we are not the geniuses of our time, but we are doing what we think is normal and reasonable. Maybe the real reason for the difference between us and other people is that when we say the sons and daughters of the UAE are our real wealth, we mean it.

You must give to be allowed to take. To accumulate talent, you must develop it; to make a good trainer, you must train someone first; to make leaders, you must coach promising talents and teach them how to avail themselves of good opportunities and avoid failure.

Human beings are the most precious asset of all nations and the most important factors in the progress of countries. We consider the development of human resources as a gauge for the development of our country. We cannot succeed in the absence of trained human resources. But, although this is the responsibility of management, it is also the responsibility of the leader because he leads the management as well as the community.

Sheikh Zayed taught us that the leader who genuinely wants to improve the status of his people realizes the importance of training human resources and equipping them with the right skills and expertise, so that they carry out their tasks efficiently and successfully. He is the one who instructs government departments to prepare and implement the plans needed to achieve these goals. Managing development is, after all, the process of managing people.

Management and leadership

The Arab philosopher Ibn Khaldoun said, "You must know that the interest subjects take in their leader does not lie in the leader's physical and intellectual abilities. This interest lies rather in what he can add to their lot in life."[3]

This, in turn, means that a leader should treat his subjects kindly, invest in their welfare and assure that the assigned management carries out its responsibilities and duties adequately; consequently, the failure of the management is the failure of the leader.

Since responsibilities are intertwined, there is no clear line between leadership and management, and a leader is more like a prime manager. Today's leadership and management experts have determined some basic differences between leaders and managers, and defined the qualities that distinguish the two, including the following examples:

- A leader leads his people while a manager leads his team.
- A leader manages the global affairs of his people, while a manager directs day-to-day affairs.
- People trust a good leader and follow the path he has drawn for them, even when they do not see where it leads. A manager must clearly show his group the path forward.
- A leader conceives a vision and outlines a strategy to implement it, while a manager is a link in the implementation process.
- A leader has a fixed position and status, while a manager can be transferred to any department.

- A leader keeps his eye on the outcomes of his effort, is concerned about their positive or negative impact on the community and eventually takes his decision based on that, while the manager protects the rules and regulations.
- A leader earns his respect and authority from his personality, capabilities and the love of people, while a manager obtains his powers from laws and authorities delegated to him.
- A leader shares his achievements with people while a manager generally monitors and controls.
- A leader dedicates his life to his people and duty, and therefore has no set working hours, while the working hours of a manager are usually fixed.
- A leader answers to his people and his conscience, while a manager answers to rules and regulations.

Based on their convictions and personal knowledge, some readers may question the validity of these differences and say that there is no way to compare a national symbol that is a leader with a manager, no matter how senior he might be. They say that the leader appoints the manager and not vice versa, and that anyone can become a manager, a minister or any other civil servant, while no one can take the place of a leader.

This is a good point if we are talking about the traditional features of a leader and of management. But since the nature of development in the UAE requires a high level of coordination, flexibility and dynamism, it requires more organization, consultation and coordination than in usual cases. This is because responsibilities might get intertwined in major projects that require common efforts and action by several departments.

Our interest in management and our consistent efforts to reform it is one of the reasons why the UAE has reached its present status in the world. Reform requires top management to reorganize its departments to serve its goals. If we do not understand this, we will keep running in circles.

When a department accepts a plan, it must use the best methods to synchronize its activities with the goals of that plan. It must also set itself clear and practical targets and stick to them. Reaching targets calls for the cooperation of all those concerned. This must involve inviting the appropriate civil servants to take part in setting those targets or at least consulting them about their validity. In explaining the targets we must ensure everybody understands them and is convinced about their validity.

Since most targets are transitional, top management should study them constantly and ensure they meet both the national goals and those of their departments. Furthermore, since most targets call for collective efforts to be successful, the department concerned should define and initiate the control system, and arrange for coordination and open lines of communication with other departments. This will ensure departmental targets are in unison with each other. Simultaneously, special attention should be given to the financial and administrative affairs within each department.

Good management

God said in his Holy Book, "One of them said O' father employ him, because the best one you can ever employ is the strong and trustworthy."[4]

Nowadays, the "strong and trustworthy" is the employee distinguished by excellence, success, commitment, honesty and good behaviour. This is the type of employee sought by leaders, managers of institutions, companies and employers in general. If management is good, employees will follow its example and distance themselves from bad colleagues even before the management dismisses the latter. If management is bad, then it corrupts others.

Government corruption obstructs foreign investment. For our part, we are providing exclusive investment opportunities that enjoy such a high reputation and we will not allow anyone to smear them. We do not have managerial corruption in the UAE – it has no place in our hearts and we simply will not stand for it. We show no compassion nor tolerance towards malfeasance, nepotism or hypocrisy.

Corrupt officials must be removed immediately and given the punishment they deserve. No one is above the law, but if some people are unafraid of it, let them at least heed God and abide by what the Prophet (PBUH) said: "A true Muslim is one who does not harm other Muslims with his tongue and his hands."[5]

Management has the specific task of faithfully serving the people and holding their interests above those of all others. There is no place in management for those who put private interests above public ones or those who favour certain people for the wrong reasons. Managers must therefore commit themselves to national goals. We expect all those who share a sound vision with us to have good character and an impeccable social behaviour.

We are talking here about highly developed professional and personal ethics that are an integral part of progress. Just like there are well-mannered employees, there are ethical companies. That is why we hear experts talking about ethical companies that are committed to values and principles – companies that will not cross the line in their behaviour.

A leader's vision is not only an economical and developmental one; it is also a social and moral one – one in which development and values need to complement each other. We must realize our goals and ambitions and implement our projects in an honest and transparent manner to us and to those working with us. In doing so, everybody will have their rightful share and God will bless our projects. Our powers are entrusted to us by our leaders to allow us to serve our people and improve their way of living. We should not accept anything else for ourselves and for all those in our society, regardless of their position.

Administrative reform

I appreciate those who speak their minds, without fear or hesitation. How can a leader learn from his mistakes if people keep telling him he was right all the time, while deep in their hearts they have another opinion? We leaders have learned to consider the words of everybody – even the man in the street. I have learned a lot from regular soldiers in our army and have often found they were right, despite their limited experience.

A leader has goals and understands the path he is travelling on. He cannot shorten the distance of the journey because that would mean diminishing the goal itself. The time we spend in studying an important matter such as performance excellence is not a waste of time but a step towards clearer goals and visions.

In the UAE, we like to treat each other as teammates with mutual respect, and encourage proactive discussion regardless of the outcome. Even if we were attending a meeting, a lecture or a seminar and this turned into a public debate, we would consider it beneficial. We believe that dialogue and an exchange of opinions are two sure ways to reach sound decisions.

Since I did not go into detail while discussing administrative behaviour, I would like to quote a hadith,[6] one of many sayings reportedly expressed by the Prophet (PBUH): "God the Almighty would love you to perfect whatever you do."[7]

In the UAE, we like to perfect whatever we do. Meetings are opportunities to discuss things, talk to each other and review our positive and negative sides. Every society has its positive and negative aspects. Right and wrong are an integral part of human behaviour. In this respect, there is no difference between an employee and the head of his department or between the latter and the leader.

Whenever somebody upsets me, I do not hide my feelings and immediately need to let the person know why I am upset. When I sleep at night, I have a sound, deep sleep because I do not entertain any evil against anyone. I like people to be frank with me and I like to be frank with them. I accept criticism because it might lead us to the right path and I expect people to accept it, just like I do, for the same reason.

Some people tell me that this or that manager works hard and is busy all the time, arriving in the office early in the morning and leaving late at night. In my opinion such a manager may not be doing a good job, despite his perseverance, if he cannot manage to develop himself and his department and improve its services and efficiency, he is underachieving and losing time.

I am not referring to any specific person in saying this, but want to say that if managers do not develop the public sector quickly, privatization will take its toll. With the exceptions of security and national defence, the private sector can assume practically all the functions of the public sector. Although the public sector may not have to compete with the private sector, the only way it can survive is through competition and through increasing its efficiency and productivity.

Public sector leaders must also get in touch with realities and open a dialogue with colleagues and businessmen, both big and small, in order to benefit from their experience and expertise. This is an ideal way to upgrade services and performance, but it needs to be done swiftly.

A manager who tries to do everything will end up doing nothing. He will find all the detours while completely losing sight of the main road. Because every project includes large and small tasks, senior managers should focus on the large ones and leave the rest to his team to handle. Upon the completion of the project, the manager should allocate some of the time he saved in assessing the performance of his team. If he cannot do this, he and his department will find themselves facing a problem they do not need.

Facilitating and complicating

Once, when I was young, a heavy panting woke me from a deep sleep in the middle of the night. I opened my eyes and saw a huge head, with two shining eyes and open jaws, looking straight at me. The head was so close to my face that its hot breath was like a blast from an oven. I was sleeping in my room at our Al Aweer[8] farm, and it was so hot that night that I had kept my window open. I then realized that the head was that of a fully-grown lion we had raised.

As the lion had grown from a young cub into adulthood, he would become difficult to control and began to attack everything he saw, whether it was a camel, a cow or a sheep. When our household could no longer handle his behaviour, they moved him to the farm. That night, the lion had thrown his full weight against the bars of his ageing cage and managed to loosen them enough to escape without the guards noticing. He had, no doubt, roamed around until he saw my open window, jumped into my bedroom and started to sniff me.

Predators can sense fear and attack frightened prey, but I knew that old lion and he knew me. I was not afraid, just annoyed, and I wanted him to leave so that I could go back to sleep. When I tried to push him out of the room through the door, he refused to leave, so I tried to push him out through the window where he had come in from, but he refused again. It then occurred to me that the best way to get rid of him was to make him imitate me by going out through the window myself. The lion fell for the trick and after he had followed me out of the window, I went back to my room, closed the window, and went back to sleep.

The simplest ways of dealing with a problem are sometimes the best. A manager can free himself from the burden of trying to do everything and not having enough time by delegating. When a leader is convinced about the benefits of delegating powers and acts accordingly, managers will follow his example. Nevertheless, you will always find managers who are reluctant to delegate some of their powers under any circumstances – rather like a conductor who wants to conduct an orchestra and play all the instruments at the same time.

Such managers ought to know that delegating power does not mean relinquishing power, abdicating one's position in favour of someone else, or losing control. Delegation of power is a way to allow managers to allocate more time for development, creativity, innovation, leadership and increasing productivity. This will allow the right team members to upgrade their capabilities and leadership skills, and build a second and third line of leaders in the division he is heading.

Some managers have discussed productivity at length and have held numerous meetings, year after year. They may even have thought they were doing their jobs quite well, until they finally realized there was no increase in productivity and little improvement in their divisions. When they asked themselves, "What went wrong?" the probable answer was that they did not develop themselves and their divisions quickly enough. They took a back seat, thinking everything was all right and left their division to manage itself.

For management to become productive, it must adopt modern management principles and set the standards for management development in the new economy, as shown in the Dubai Government Excellence Programme. If those standards are introduced properly, they can secure success at the departmental level and in the country as a whole.

I have instructed various departments of the government to follow the quality standards set by the programme to develop their regulations, upgrade their services and strengths, and avoid performance pitfalls. The next step is the implementation of the Dubai e-government plan, in addition to plans and projects that are already in place and others that are still in the planning stages.

In a previous chapter, I suggested that practicality is one of the preconditions for a vision to materialize. This implies that its goals should be realistic and feasible, because dreams and desires that do not take root in the real world are not the kind of goals we are thinking about. The rest must be transformed into a well-organized working plan supervised by professionals. Such plans, as well as those in charge of implementing them, should be subject to evaluation and follow-up, and be held accountable to make sure the speed of implementation matches the speed of the new global economy.

Some might say that the UAE is not the only country with unique, practical development visions, or the only one to set standards or set itself goals. So what distinguishes it from others? I believe that one of the differences lies in our definition of reality. In our opinion, reality is not the present one but the one we feel should exist.

If we say, for example, that the goal of our administrative reforms and upgrading our management's performance is to develop the government's performance in a short time, to a level matching the service quality and productivity methods of the private sector, would this proposal be realistic?

While this may be considered as wishful thinking even in some advanced countries, for us it is a 100-per cent realistic goal.

We have another realistic goal – one that I believe is more like a dream for others – and that is to raise the standards of the public sector's services, efficiency and performance, to levels superior to those of the private sector. We do not want to move the clock's hands backwards and substitute the private sector with the public sector; on the contrary, we want to usher the private sector into a new era of excellence, efficiency and performance.

The word 'race' has appeared a number of times in this book and I will not stop repeating it, because it summarizes all the developments currently taking place in our world. Time is passing, the clock is ticking, the world is racing, and no one will wait for us. We cannot ask our competitors to wait; we must rather develop and enhance our performance and ourselves.

We cannot stop now. I did not begin my book with the tale of the lion and the gazelle for no reason. I was not really telling a tale but issuing a warning, one which I am the first to heed. In brief, it reminds us that if we were gazelles and stopped running, lions would devour us; and if we were lions and stopped running, we would starve to death.

Do we have any other alternative?

---

1 Dubai Government Excellence Programme aims to bring about a qualitative leap in the performance of Dubai's public sector through self-assessment processes, according to recognized evaluation standards.

2 *Musnad Ahmad Ibn Hanbal*, narrated by Ahmad Ibn Mohammed Ibn Hanbal and freely translated from the Arabic.

3 Ibn Khaldoun, *The Muqaddimah of Ibn Khaldoun*, Beirut: Al Hilal, p. 129.

4 Sura Al Qasas, v. 26.

5 *Sahih Muslim*, narrated by Muslim Ibn Al Hajjaj Al Nisaburi and freely translated from the Arabic.

6 A collection of traditions containing the sayings of the Prophet Mohammed (PBUH), with accounts of his daily practice, that constitute the major source of guidance for Muslims apart from the Qur'an.

7 *Shu'ab al-Iman (The Branches of Faith)*, narrated by Ahmad Ibn Husayn Al Bayhaqi and freely translated from the Arabic.

8 Al Aweer is a suburb of Dubai, about 35 kilometres from the city. It was a farming village with Bedouin camps until the 1990s, when the city expanded on a large scale.

CHAPTER FIVE

Decision-making and Teamwork

Making the right decision at the right moment is one of the most important factors for success.

Making such decisions is also one of the most important responsibilities of true leaders, because it calls for daring, willpower, a quick response and a deep awareness of the consequences of the decisions and how they will fit into the leader's goals.

By making the right decision at the right moment, a leader can tip the balance between success and failure, overtake others, make something out of nothing and improve the lot of his people, while earning the respect of others.

Leadership is all about being capable of making decisions, and successful leadership is all about making successful decisions. The higher the quality of information on which the leader bases his decision, the higher the chances are that his decision will be the right one. Deep consideration, consultation, research and thinking are all needed in reaching the right decision. If a leader fails to turn his vision into a decision and that decision into reality, then he is a failure.

To avoid failure, a leader must develop his vision according to a strict timetable, because delay and procrastination are the enemies of success. When we review history, we find that many leaders lost crucial battles because they did not make the right decisions at the right time; when they finally did, it was too late – the situation had changed and potential victories turned into defeats.

Behind every major failure lies a failed decision, and behind every failed decision lies a government that failed its people – a government that did not carry out its duties properly, having made the wrong decisions or delaying the right ones.

How can a leader avoid making wrong decisions?

He should carefully consider his goals when taking a decision and examine the potential benefits and risks. If there are risks, the odds and alternatives should be taken into consideration. There should be no dark areas and the road forward should be absolutely clear for each and every step. This calls for a quiet and careful study of each aspect of the decision and taking the advice of experts into consideration, as well as the lessons learned from previous experience.

In Dubai, we do not take any decisions unless we are totally confident about the feasibility of the project and our ability to assimilate and market it. But whenever we launch a new project, we never stop until it is completed. All this happens quickly and efficiently, under the control of competent people. Arrogance, bias and favouritism are not the right ingredients for taking the right decision. To succeed, you must research, plan and prepare to proceed with the right decision.

Conceive then proceed – never leave anything to chance or count on favourable winds, unless they are actually blowing.

There is a famous Arab poem that states that winds do not always provide what ships need. When there is a gale, your ship had better be safely moored and not remain on the high seas. If you were at sea, you would need to know exactly what to do, having considered in advance all the potential contingencies that might occur and the way out of them. Leave yourself some options, and be flexible, not obstinate.

Some decisions are easy to make and come naturally in the normal course of work. Any official can take such a decision anytime, but a leader must always be prepared to take the most difficult decisions to achieve specific goals, and often, at very short notice if not immediately. Although I cannot list all the difficult decisions I have taken throughout my life – some of which are beyond the realm of this book – I would like to provide two examples.

During the Gulf War[1] in 1991, there were air raids and missile attacks on ships and aircraft, to the extent that insurance companies decided to stop insuring air and sea freight in our region. We immediately responded with a decision to insure our air routes and shipping lanes ourselves. This ensured business carried on as usual for airfreight and shipping, and that freight kept moving through our ports and airports to their final destinations in the Gulf. This courageous decision not only benefited our country but greatly enhanced our prestige.

The second example of one of the most difficult decisions I have taken in my life was the announcement of an AED 55 billion (US$15 billion) deal to purchase fifty-eight modern jet aircraft to bolster the fleet of Emirates Airline. The deal was announced during the Dubai Air Show[2] in November 2001. Many questioned the wisdom of such a decision just two months after the terrible 9/11 attacks on New York. Those attacks were followed by a crisis in the airline industry, especially in the US and Europe, with a number of airlines going bankrupt.

There were those who questioned the wisdom of that decision but my vision for the future was my prime motive. I knew that this was a rare opportunity to purchase jet aircraft at the prevailing low prices and that we would definitely need those jets in the future. Furthermore, the deal was bound to promote international confidence in Emirates Airline and its capacity to fly more passengers when the market picked up, following the transitory recession in the world economy.

We took the right decision and time did not only prove us right, it also proved our timing was right.

Some decisions are taken within the context of others with broader scope and having even more futuristic goals. When, for example, Emirates Airlines launched its Dubai–Osaka flights, Fusae Ohta, the former Mayor of Osaka, told me that these flights would soon reach maximum capacity. I agreed and added that I did not want to take into consideration what would happen immediately after launching the flights, but was more interested in what would happen one and a half years after the launch.

Such decisions involve risks, but since we consider ourselves the custodians of our people's interests and the welfare of this country, and since anything that is good for this country will also benefit its people, we must always strive to promote that good – even if it involves risks.

This calls for utmost care, because it is true that the higher the risks, the greater the reward. For our part, we take calculated risks only after fully considering the situation. We also avoid all those risks where we are unable to ascertain where they will lead our country, our people and our economy.

Not all decisions and risks are the same. These rank on several levels, each one of which requires a detailed study and must be based on a fully comprehensive plan. The plan must, in its turn, cover the subject matter, the person in charge of the implementation of the project, the timetable, the person in charge of the follow-up, and the various alternatives available to us. This does not mean we will not make mistakes, but mistakes have never caused any of our projects to fail.

I can provide many examples about decisions that were implemented and resulted in successful ventures, including our first championship golf course and the launching of Dubai Internet City and Dubai Media City. Even the projects that were criticized and expected by some to fail succeeded. Take The Palm Jumeirah for example. All the island's housing units were sold in seventy-two hours, before even one wall was built. We opted to settle for a smaller profit margin in order to make the properties more affordable to a larger segment of the market.

A leader should not try to convince his people that he is working for their good just by taking decisions that eventually benefit them. A leader should rather focus on making his people see tangible results through projects that do just that. When a leader succeeds in distributing wealth to a large number of people, he will motivate them to spend more and speed up the economic cycle. Working for the good of the people also implies working for the good of the business community, because it is the very pillar of the national economy.

The stronger the pillar, the stronger and more satisfied the people. The more satisfied the people, the more focused they will be on building up national wealth. And the more focused on building up national wealth they are, the stronger and the more capable the government will be in taking the right decisions. This, in turn, contributes to building the national wealth. It is a continuous cycle that benefits everyone once it is properly linked. But once it is cut, everyone suffers.

When people ask me about the project closest to my heart, I always tell them that it depends on the location, the date and the nature of the project. For me, a project is like having a child – one who I like to stay close to, work for, care about, nurture and oversee till maturity. Then a new project comes along and the whole cycle repeats itself.

Teamwork

Some people say Arabs make good individuals but bad working teams, and that is why we suffer from bad management and weak institutions. I believe that this is an unfair generalization. Building a civilization requires a joint effort and Arabs are heirs to a great civilization, so they must certainly have been able to work together.

But even if we set civilization aside for a few moments, we will find that teamwork in fields such as farming, hunting and building was vital for the survival of our species since the dawn of time.

We all know how successful our forefathers were in their pearl-diving days[3]. Those arduous voyages were a good example of people who realized the importance of teamwork. Each individual on board the dhows that roamed the pearl banks of the Gulf had a specific task to carry out at the right moment and as best he could. The divers' lives depended on it. Concerted effort was the prerequisite for sailing home after a long and painstaking time at sea with a good harvest of pearls. Individualism at best would have meant a loss of profit, at worst, death.

Teamwork is obviously the major driving force of any great undertaking. When each member of a team fully understands his part, he feels more committed to the team and more determined to provide his best. Our economy today is more complicated and diversified than that of yesterday. To realize our common goals in today's complex economic scene, we need a higher level of coordination, not only by members of individual teams, but also on a collective level.

Teamwork is one of the most important ways to successfully realize a leader's vision and its goals. One successful leader was once quoted as saying, "I want team members who love winning and hate losing". Even if the leaders cannot find the right team members, they should select the best available ones and coach them to success.

A team should not only be distinguished in its work, but also in its thinking and behaviour. It must also have confidence in itself and in other teams, because this promotes better commitment. A team member might have his own foresight and ambition driving him to excel in his work, but all team members must have confidence in the leader's vision, think positively about it and work together to achieve its goals.

An efficient team would ideally be built on mutual trust, commitment, close cooperation, good communication and clearly set goals. Team members should be respected, appreciated, encouraged, motivated and enjoy shared responsibilities. There are several methods to achieve this, the most important of which is to let team members contribute to the different stages of the project, starting from the design stage, and delegating them with the necessary powers to implement it.

The most important element in delegating power is for the leader to choose the right people. After all, the leader has to bear full responsibility for his decisions. Delegating some power does not relieve the leader of all his responsibilities, even if the official to whom he delegated that power was the one at fault. Delegation of power is temporary by nature, and restricted to a specific project or task. It is certainly not an abdication of responsibilities.

Obviously, a leader should not just delegate power and then forget all about the task. He needs to regularly follow up on the work being done and intervene, if necessary, to correct any irregularities or provide advice. The empowered official, on the other hand, needs to be fully aware that the powers entrusted to him can be withdrawn at any time.

Despite the above, the delegation of powers definitely involves risk. When we began conceiving the Dubai e-government project, for example, I could have selected an executive team from my best heads of departments – people who are known for their efficiency – but I did not. Since the project was crucial in making Dubai an international centre for the new global economy, and involved applying the latest technologies for upgrading performance, services and productivity, I decided to choose the members of the executive team from the backbenches. I picked a team of very efficient people, confident in their ability to successfully realize the project, not only on schedule but in record time.

At all times, I keep one eye on promising staff and the other on opportunities – opportunities that will provide them with the chance to show their full potential. Once an opportunity appears, I empower these people to do the job and expect them to proceed as quickly as possible.

If these people pass the test with high marks and their performance meets my expectations, I may promote them to senior executive posts and entrust them to oversee one or more projects. I take great care, during that sensitive period of the development of a person's leadership skills, to provide all the cooperation, support and encouragement needed.

The most important factor in this process is that the leader should be ready to take responsibility for any mistake the empowered person might make, together with the consequences thereof.

In order to avoid problems, some leaders restrict their search for good candidates to experienced ministers, undersecretaries and senior managers. But this is not the way true leaders are made. If in Dubai we had not delegated power, had not shouldered responsibility for the decisions and actions of those whom we have empowered, and had not followed up on their performances, we would not have had so many young and successful executives to be proud of.

The expertise and capabilities of our new generation of executives match those of the world's finest executive teams. If we had not discovered and coached these bright young people, they would probably have remained restricted to their routine daily tasks, instead of displaying their creativity, enthusiasm and ability to excel. If we carry on discovering hidden talent, and allow their leadership potential to blossom, we will promote their peace of mind, self-confidence and trust in others.

This, in turn, will promote the concept and spirit of teamwork. It will also show the need for concerted efforts and mutual support by team members. This is crucial for the success of teamwork, and each team member must be exactly aware of his or her role in this. Reaching a high level of coordination is an expertise team members need to acquire through consistent training and learning. Management studies have special courses dedicated to training. They teach you how to make your team accept you and how to be an efficient member of your team.

The leader and the team

We are all soldiers in the development army and have the same ranks and tasks that exist in traditional armies. Work teams are in the front line of development and are entrusted only to the most crucial missions – those that can secure victory in the development war. Unless the leader of these teams provides them with the right training, incentives, care and encouragement, and unless he is leading them, they will never be able to conquer obstacles and achieve their goals.

I have previously said leadership is one of the most difficult topics to explain, especially since my own experiences were the only references I had in writing this book. I would like to add that exercising leadership is just as difficult.

Many people have asked what the most difficult obstacle I have faced during the last twenty years was. This book provides the perfect opportunity to respond.

The biggest obstacle I have ever encountered in my drive to develop my country was to know how to convey the message to those in charge of the development process, so that they understood precisely what I wanted them to do. It was making sure that all those working with me understood my vision, so that they could work to achieve its goals, recognize its path and have each and every stage clear in their minds. This was crucial for sticking to the goals.

This obstacle was not at all restricted only to those I deal with in the public sector. It was a tremendous effort, but in the end, everyone understood their tasks and proceeded to execute them. Now that we are all in the race, I consider this achievement my greatest reward.

Although leadership is very difficult, I enjoy my work and always make sure that my team enjoys it as well. Those who do not enjoy their work are not very productive.

---

1 The Gulf War, codenamed Operation Desert Storm (17 January 1991–28 February 1991) was a war waged by a UN-authorized coalition force from thirty-four nations led by the United States, against Iraq in response to Iraq's invasion and annexation of Kuwait.

2 The Dubai Airshow is a biennial show organized by F&E Aerospace since 1989, in cooperation with the Government of Dubai, the Dubai Civil Aviation Authority, Dubai Airports and in collaboration with the UAE Armed Forces.

3 Until the 1930s, the pearling industry was, apart from trading, the only source of income for the people living in the region now known as the UAE. The industry collapsed as a direct result of the worldwide economic depression and the introduction of the Japanese cultured pearl.

Part III

DEVELOPMENT FOR SURVIVAL

CHAPTER SIX

The Banks of the Creek

The struggle for survival

The pearl industry was the backbone of the economies of the Gulf states in general and of Dubai in particular. A substantial number of the region's population was engaged in the pearl harvest or involved in professions related to trading in pearls. Pearl trading prospered so much in Dubai, that it became one of the Gulf's major trading centres for this precious commodity.

Although diving for pearls brought some relief to the region's population, it involved unbearable difficulty and suffering. Divers and sailors suffered the most in what amounted to a ferocious battle to earn a living for their families. But the people of the region were steadfast in this harsh struggle for survival and suffered its calamities without flinching.

When young Gulf citizens hear the stories of what their fathers and grandfathers had to endure to survive, they think they are the stuff legends are made of. They cannot believe that those tales of suffering are true because nowadays, they have all the luxuries of modern civilization and cannot imagine anything else. I still remember how deeply I was touched whenever I heard about the suffering of divers. We must remember them with gratitude and appreciation, and be proud to be the descendants of such great people – people who overcame immense challenges.

The pearl crisis

Throughout its history, the Gulf region, including the area that is now known as the United Arab Emirates, played an extremely important role in world trade, as an important transit point for sea cargoes and desert caravans.

The rulers of Dubai contributed to the stability of the emirate and the prosperity of its trade, by opening its doors to foreign traders and entrepreneurs, and providing them with a variety of facilities. This wise policy bore fruit, had a positive impact on the emirate's economy, and earned Dubai its dominant trading status in the region.

Dubai's prominence in the pearl trade allowed its economy to prosper and transformed the emirate into an important regional centre for producing and marketing pearls. It was therefore only natural that Dubai suffered more than other Gulf cities from the collapse in demand for natural pearls. This was a consequence of the worldwide Great Depression of the early 1930s and the introduction of the cheaper Japanese cultured pearl at the same time. People all over the region suffered from the loss of their major source of income and regional trade fell sharply.

Because of the Great Depression, international trade also fell by more than half its pre-recession value and the global economy slumped into decline. Factories shut down all around the world and hundreds of thousands of people lost their jobs.

When people cannot afford even the bare necessities, they obviously cannot afford luxuries. The global demand for a broad range of luxury goods, including natural pearls from the Gulf, fell dramatically. Some countries even banned the importing of luxury goods altogether because of the collapse of their currencies. But the most deadly blow to hit the Gulf pearl was the cultured pearl. Despite being very difficult to differentiate from natural pearls outside of a laboratory, the cultured pearls were considerably cheaper than their natural counterparts.

With the demise of the mainstay of the Gulf's economy, the people in Dubai and other Gulf cities suffered an extended economic recession. The years that followed the crash of the pearl trade were some of the most challenging in the whole region, and Dubai was not excluded. People had depended heavily on the pearl trade, and its demise led to mass bankruptcies and unspeakable hardship. Yet the region's population in general, and that of Dubai in particular, was so resilient, so accustomed to hardship, and so confident in God's mercy – and in themselves – that they managed to survive the recession.

Many traders successfully shifted to trading in other goods and the diving dhows were transformed into cargo and passenger vessels, while divers tried to scrape a living by fishing, farming and all other sorts of menial jobs. Dubai was more fortunate because of the strategic location of its natural harbour, the Creek,[1] and the enlightened economic policies of its rulers. It consequently managed to attract more ships, trade, traders and entrepreneurs than others. Like a phoenix rising from the ashes, the pearl-dependent economy diversified into all sorts of other trades and ventures, allowing the emirate to prosper again and become the unchallenged hub of Gulf trade.

The search for alternatives

They say that throughout human history, achievements were the products of dreams and ideas. In the following chapters, I will attempt to shed more light on the goals of the dreams, visions and ideas that shaped the region until the middle of this century and thereafter.

Dubai is determined to promote its international competitive edge. We are indeed competitive, thanks to our strategic East–West location, our sophisticated infrastructure and our tax-free economy that offers investors quality, cost-efficiency and minimum bureaucracy.

Such economic concepts look very modern indeed and a tax-free economy is not only ahead of its time now, but will remain so in the foreseeable future. Regardless of their sophistication and development levels, most countries have, to date, failed to reach an economic formula that allows them to even consider abolishing taxes. If we want to be more realistic, we must admit that taxation has become something of a self-perpetuating industry in many countries. Ever since the end of the Second World War, this industry has never stopped growing and is now generating all sorts of systems and rules that affect all aspects of human life.

Some tax systems have become so complicated that many Westerners cannot complete their annual tax returns without the help of a chartered accountant. If today a tax-free economy is viewed as progressive and ahead of its time, consider how advanced this economic concept would have been 100 years ago?

Although I am using the latest terminology while writing about the concept of a modern tax-free economy, I sometimes feel that I am merely repeating concepts Dubai knew a century before the WTO was established. Such concepts were among the most important reasons for Dubai's prominence in the trade arena.

In 1902, following an increase in taxation across the Gulf at the Persian port of Lingeh, Sheikh Maktoum bin Hasher[2], the Ruler of Dubai at the time, abolished all custom duties on imports. As a result of Sheikh Maktoum's liberal policy, Indian goods flooded into the city's port shortly thereafter and Dubai soon became the Gulf's hub for re-export to neighbouring ports or inland markets, such as the Buraimi Oasis.[3] A large number of prominent Gulf merchants soon moved to Dubai and made it their regional headquarters.

Sheikh Maktoum's successor, my grandfather, Sheikh Saeed bin Maktoum[4], continued to adopt open economic policies and free trade from all sorts of duties, including those previously imposed on the export of pearls, the largest trade segment by far at the time. This contributed to Dubai's growing prosperity and allowed the city to become one of the region's most important pearl-trading centres.

Although the UAE was one of the largest beneficiaries of that trade in the Gulf region, it was similarly one of the hardest hit by its demise.

Dubai entertained other economic activities at the time, a large part of which was in one way or another related to servicing the pearl trade. During the seventeen years between the start of the Great Depression of 1929 and the end of the Second World War in 1945, the emirate searched for alternatives to the pearl trade and did not leave a single stone unturned in an effort to sustain its economy and provide its residents with basic services.

In 1937 Sheikh Saeed signed a sole proprietorship agreement for oil exploration with the Trucial States Petroleum Company[5]. The agreement with the company, which was affiliated with the Iraq Oil Company, took twenty months to negotiate and granted the exploration rights for seventy-five years against an annual royalty of 30,000 Indian rupees.

Dubai had high hopes of discovering oil in its territories, especially when the company promised to pay the Government of Dubai 200,000 rupees within two months of discovering oil in commercial quantities, in addition to three rupees against each exported barrel of oil. Unfortunately, the company failed to find oil and relinquished its concession.

Dubai had no other option but to resume focusing on what it knew best: trade in general and re-export in particular. Traders used to import duty-free goods to Dubai in bulk quantities at competitive prices and re-export them tax-free to the region's markets. Gold was the most important re-export item from Dubai, especially after the Second World War, and picked up sharply when many countries in the region banned its import for economic reasons.

The Government of Dubai strongly supported the re-export trade by building a modern international airport in 1959 and deepening and developing the city's natural creek, which was and still is one of its major economic resources. With time, and having accumulated sufficient experience and expertise, Dubai became one of the foremost gold re-exporting centres and the favourite regional headquarters for a large number of banks and companies involved in marketing the precious metal.

Praise and criticism

I once rushed to my father, enraged, and told him about certain newspapers that were publishing false stories about Dubai, suggesting that he prohibited the sale of those newspapers in the emirate. My father calmed me down and explained that it was better to allow them access to our city, so that if what they were publishing was true, we deserved the criticism; and if not, nobody would believe them. I left convinced of his wisdom and determined never to ban any publication under any circumstances.

I prefer to see constructive criticism in the press rather than praise. Everyone knows about achievements and we do not really need any reminders, but uncovering mistakes leads officials and decision-makers to correct them and avoid making more. I never try to impose or imply to the press what they should be writing and publishing, because media professionals know their jobs better than I do. What I always wish, however, is for criticism to be accurate and supported with content that is the result of professional research, and not originating from dubious sources, rumours or insinuations.

Reverting to the re-export of gold, this preamble was necessary to advise those who said or implied that the Government of Dubai once encouraged gold smuggling into the Indian subcontinent, that their allegations were unfounded. What really happened was that gold was legally imported into the emirate, according to agreements concluded between the banks, companies selling the gold and local traders, and was re-exported legally as well. How the gold was managed after leaving the borders of the emirate was not its responsibility.

Great Britain remained in the Trucial States until 1971 and investigated complaints about gold smuggling, but never found any justification to stop its trade, because it had established the legality of that trade. Nevertheless, and although we have to acknowledge the role gold played in Dubai's re-export trade in the 1950s and 1960s, it should also be said that it was not the only commodity re-exported from Dubai's ports at the time. Hundreds of other goods and commodities were also shipped to other Gulf countries, Iran, Iraq, the Indian subcontinent and East Africa.

Everyone must also be aware that the real fact redeeming Dubai after the crash of the pearl trade was neither gold at the time, nor oil afterwards, nor any other commodity. What really saved the day was the foresight and vision Dubai's rulers had exhibited since the end of the nineteenth century.

Dubai's current development drive is not a policy we chose from a list of various alternatives available to us. It is not a policy my father, grandfather and forefathers opted for in the past among other alternatives. It is an integral part of Dubai's constitution and set in the minds of its leaders. It is the most effective weapon in our struggle for survival. As it was in the past and will be in the future, is the only option capable of ascertaining Dubai's continuity and development.

Our development method is the only way to avoid the side effects of economic shocks in the East and West. It is a method based on the principles of free trade, open markets and skies, and a tax-free economic system. The interaction between these principles with the high skills and expertise of Dubai's traders, and the cooperation of all its people, is the true maker of this great opportunity and puts the emirate in a leading commercial and economic position in the Gulf.

Modern Dubai

There is no specific date for the beginning of the rise of modern Dubai. The search for alternatives for the defunct pearl trade never stopped and development was taking place when my grandfather died and my father took over the reins of power in 1958. However, one crucial turning point in Dubai's modern history was the dredging of the Creek in 1960.

The British say, "Any port in a storm." No captain would wish for a safer and more secure port than Dubai Creek. This fourteen-kilometre waterway is one of the best natural harbours in the Gulf, if not in the world. It is therefore only natural that the Creek shaped Dubai and became the source of its survival, distinction and growth over the years. It is the very heart and soul of Dubai – its raison d'être.

The Creek was an excellent harbour for small- and medium-sized dhows that moored along its banks, to offload as much as 300 tonnes of goods and sail back to India or East Africa loaded with all sorts of other goods. The boom in shipping after the Second World War, using large, motorized merchant ships, forced these ships to moor outside the Creek, which could not accommodate their deeper draft. Goods were then transhipped onto and from barges that were able to navigate the Creek's shallow waters.

This handicap slowed shipping and raised its costs, to a point that forced my father, who was then the Crown Prince of Dubai, to search for a solution. In 1954 he commissioned a feasibility study for dredging the Creek. Since the government could not finance the project on its own, my father established a special fund to which a local bank contributed £200,000, while Kuwait contributed a £400,000 loan.

The Creek was then dredged and provided with two long berths along its banks, and with a bridge linking them by land – the Al Maktoum Bridge which opened to traffic in 1963. Simultaneously, my father, entertaining renewed hopes of discovering oil, established two companies to search for oil in the emirate in 1963. The two companies, Dubai Petroleum and Dubai Offshore Operating Company Limited, went into partnership with several foreign companies that divided the onshore and offshore concessions between themselves.

This time oil was discovered at the Fateh field in 1966. There was another oil strike at the South-West Fateh field four years later, in addition to those at two more fields, Falah and Rashid. All these fields were situated offshore.

The companies in charge of production faced a problem storing the extracted oil because of the shallow water in the discovery area. They soon improvised with the pioneering idea of manufacturing huge floating tanks in Dubai and towing them to the production site to store the oil and pump it into oil tankers for export. The first shipment left the Fateh field on 22 September 1969, allowing the emirate to finance its ambitious development plans and usher in a new stage in its history, with several mega projects, the likes of which the Gulf and the Middle East regions had never witnessed before.

Following the deepening and widening of the Creek, ships loaded with up to 800 tonnes of goods were able to use the new berthing facilities and trade prospered. My father expected Dubai would soon attract much more trade and with the Creek being full to capacity, he decided that much larger port facilities in deeper water were needed.

In 1969, he ordered the construction of Port Rashid with four berths, but long before they were completed, he ordered the construction company to add eleven more berths. The first phase of the port was completed in 1972 and was followed by an expansion project in 1978 that raised the total number of berths to thirty-five, five of which could accommodate the world's largest container ships of the time. Then, just two years before the completion of the expansion project, my father surprised everybody by ordering the construction of a large new port. That was the Port of Jebel Ali, which was equipped with twice as many berths as Port Rashid, and with a huge shipyard for ship maintenance.

The year 1979 is considered by many as being especially significant in Dubai's history, since three of the emirate's largest projects were commissioned that year.

The first of these projects was the Port of Jebel Ali. The second was the aluminium smelter constructed and owned by Dubai Aluminium Company (DUBAL), with an initial annual capacity of 135,000 tonnes. The third mega project commissioned that year was the Dubai International Trade Centre (now known as the Dubai World Trade Centre), the tallest building in the Middle East at the time and one of the world's largest. At that early date my father equipped the people of Dubai with a unique infrastructure and a successful industrial base that immediately transformed the emirate into a prominent regional business centre.

Development and optimism

Exactly what is it that Dubai has to its advantage? If the weather, desert, sandy beaches and sea do not create development, what does?

Only people can make development happen. The secret of successful development lies in reaching an ideal formula that can efficiently use the skills of people along with, in Dubai's case, the existence of the Creek, sunny skies, desert, sandy beaches and sea, to put in place a uniquely successful metropolis. The context of this formula is the right vision and the key to its success is the leader, who combines his goals and determination to see them through to fruition, despite all obstacles.

I believe my father had a third edge that helped him succeed: the absence of any delineating line between his goals and their implementation. These two factors were one and the same for him, and they were engaged in a constant race with time and competition. This explains why he always realized his projects in record time, despite the huge challenges he faced with each one of them, and why all his projects were as successful as he had expected.

Anyone looking back to the period when Dubai's mega projects were being implemented, and then looking at the early 1980s, when the Gulf's economy blossomed, is bound to discover a clear relationship between the boom in projects and the boom in the development that followed. But how could my father have predicted so precisely in the 1970s what the 1980s would bring?

Let us see what happened in the 1970s first. The price of oil was around US$2 per barrel, when the first stage of the Port Rashid project was commissioned. But the price kept climbing throughout the 1970s to reach US$38 by 1982. This sharply rising oil income explains the unprecedented and extensive growth the Gulf economies witnessed during those years. When those mega projects were commissioned, Dubai was in an ideal position to undertaken them.

Rising demand for aluminium for example, drove the Dubai Aluminium Company (DUBAL) to raise its production to more than 151,000 tonnes by 1983. The proceeds of exporting this amount of aluminium stood at AED 460 million (US$125 million) and represented about half of Dubai's non-oil exports at the time. Ever since, DUBAL has kept expanding its production capacities, reaching 722,000 tonnes in 2005.

My father had another remarkable quality – optimism. No leader, how confident he might be in his goals, can embark on the huge risks my father took in implementing his legendary multi-billion-dollar projects, if optimism was not a major part of his vision. He was intent on succeeding and remained an optimist even when pessimism was the prevailing mood mindset in the region, and even when the staunchest of investors kept away from looming risks, in an environment full of gloom and fear. Not surprisingly, optimism is another thing I learned from my father: optimism about the future and the people of Dubai, the UAE, the Gulf and the whole Arab world.

I believe that true social stability is closely linked to economic stability. I also believe that the final goal of any sound economic development exercise should be the survival of the people and the country, and providing these people with security and amenities and motivating them to build their own fortunes.

These are the same goals we are striving to achieve today, armed with the same determination to succeed, the same confidence in the vision and the people, and the same optimism and persistence in taking Dubai's unique development process ever further. This is the kind of continuity Dubai is accustomed to.

My father lived through the economic crisis following the crash of the pearl trade and witnessed the bitter hardships people endured. He was therefore fully aware of the meaning of living in deprivation and backwardness. He wanted to improve the standards of living of his people, because he was aware of their great suffering. This was the only thing motivating my father's thoughts. He wanted to keep hunger, need and backwardness away from Dubai's shores forever.

All that we have done in Dubai so far – and will do in the future – is to stay on the course of development my father embarked on. The most important difference, however, between old days and the present, is that we will need an even wider road – the widest possible to allow the new-world economy access to our shores. This calls for implementing our strategic economic diversification policies, laying solid foundations for excellence and prosperity, and transforming Dubai from a regional trade centre into an international finance, services and electronic trade centre.

Trade and services were the foundation blocks of my father's development goals. He must have foreseen the need for them. He was determined to develop these two industries and find the necessary finance, regardless of the results of oil exploration.

By the end of 1984, the oil exploration concessions in the emirate covered 10,000 square kilometres. Seven international groups were pumping around 324,000 barrels of oil a day from some 200 wells. This included the Murgham onshore field, which was connected to the Jebel Ali area with a 65-kilometre pipeline. The following year, the emirate's oil production rose to 348,000 barrels of oil a day and peaked at 400,000 barrels, before gradually declining.

Our economy is nevertheless growing continuously, because we have succeeded in bolstering the non-oil sectors and developing new industries, which generated US$37 billion (AED 136 billion) in 2005 and represented some 94 per cent of our GDP.

I must take this opportunity to acknowledge with gratitude the support provided by Sheikh Zayed. Without Sheikh Zayed, Dubai would not have been able to reach its current commercial and economic status. He unconditionally supported Dubai's development efforts, out of his unflinching confidence in the future and the success of the Federation. He never hesitated even for a second in fully supporting any effort to promote the status of the UAE on the world's economic map.

Sheikh Zayed did all this and more, through fairness, consultation, honesty, strong work ethic, dedication to serving the people and the country and by focusing on enlightened development. He opened a door on the world – an action that enabled the UAE to rank among the world's most advanced nations in record speed. I am confident that he left us in the knowledge of the great value of his achievements, which compare with those of other great men in history.

My father faced formidable challenges throughout his life, which he managed to overcome with the help of God and his own unflinching determination. With God's help, we will follow in his footsteps.

There was a time we used to worry about the aftermath of the depletion of our oil resources, but these worries are dissipating. We have successfully diversified our economy by focusing on trade, tourism, services and creating new opportunities. We have succeeded because we mastered the art of exploiting the best resource in the world for acquiring inexhaustible riches. I will discuss this in more detail in the following chapters of the book.

---

1 Dubai Creek or Khor Dubai is a saltwater creek located in Dubai, UAE. It ends at Ras Al Khor Wildlife Sanctuary.

2 Sheikh Maktoum bin Hasher Al Maktoum was the Ruler of Dubai from 1894 until his death in 1906.

3 Buraimi Oasis or Al Buraymi is an oasis town in northeastern Oman, on the border of the UAE.

4 Sheikh Saeed bin Maktoum Al Maktoum (born 1878) was the Ruler of Dubai from 1912 until his death in 1958.

5 The Trucial States is the former name for the region now known as the UAE. The term 'trucial' refers to the maritime truces concluded between Great Britain and the rulers of the region's sheikhdoms during the nineteenth century.

CHAPTER SEVEN

Minding the Minds

What I wish most for the youth of the United Arab Emirates is success.

I am proud of everyone who has worked to achieve our goals. All I want now is for each one of our young men and women to make their own success story – the story they deserve, one that allows them to raise their heads high and tell themselves, their family and their friends, "I am proud of what I have accomplished."

With the help of God, we can realize our immediate ambitions. One day in the future I want all these young people to look around, see the heights the UAE has reached and tell their children, "I was part of this and I would like you and your children to continue the work for the sake of all Arabs."

I am a brother to all my people. A true brother is one who tries to help his siblings advance and this is what I always strive for. We are also partners on the road to development and excellence; in our vision, interests and destiny; in our past, present and future achievements.

I spoke about vision and dreams in a previous chapter and attempted to explain the difference between them, through the realistic quality of the first and the imaginative character of the second. I would not, however, like anyone to conclude that I am against dreams. Life itself is a big dream and people dream each day of their lives.

Effort, work, planning and preparation are the tools needed to realize dreams and their goals. If dreams are the cornerstone of great ideas, creativity is their foundation. Contrary to what many failed Arab managers claim, I believe that the failure of Arab management does not lie in the individualistic nature of Arabs, but is the result of oppressing this individualism.

When we allow individuals to be themselves and practise their individuality, we free their potential and motivate their creativity.

Where is the wisdom in restricting action and stifling creativity? We all claim we want to develop the individual in order to pave the way for the development of the whole nation. But where in the Arab world do we see institutes and establishments that contribute to promoting and motivating creativity in young people? Where is the appropriate training? Where is the encouragement? And where is the motivation?

Our experience in the UAE has taught us that there are no big secrets in the development process. The quality of a group is derived from the quality of its members, and the strength of a community is derived from the strength of its sons and daughters. When we free the potential of individuals, we simultaneously free the potential of the whole community they are part of, and when we let the creativity of individuals blossom, the creativity of the community as a whole blossoms.

This is no big secret. When we are facing development issues that need us to run in order to successfully face them, how can I expect anyone to run if I keep putting obstacles in their way? Where is the proper development track in the Arab world? What is the use of encouraging a soldier to fight when you have not trained and armed him properly?

Some leaders have reached the point of being unable able to thank those working with them, and some do not even know how to pat a successful man on the shoulder and tell him, "Well done, you have accomplished something and should be rewarded!"

Do these leaders know the impact a kind word can have – that it is the bridge to hearts, the way to raise morale and remove any misunderstanding? We all have to master how to say these words spontaneously and with sincerity. This is also true for smiles and personal touches that show we care about the well-being of those that depend on us and that we have an interest in solving their problems.

These leaders should be aware of what motivation can do. It boosts the potential of young people, enhances their dedication and drives them to succeed and achieve for generations. It is a proven and inexpensive way to earn loyalty while increasing productivity. It is a behaviour every successful leader should adopt in dealing with people and encourage others to do the same. It is, moreover, a civilized behaviour that the whole community should adopt.

Some leaders have tried to use fear instead of this. They feel individuals should be afraid of their leaders and of their power over them. This leads employees to wrongly believe that if they work, they will make mistakes and be punished; if they do not work, they will not make mistakes and will not be punished.

We in the Arab world cannot realize our ambitions, complete huge projects and generate millions of job opportunities if individuals and communities are subdued this way. When this happens, the community will simply not cooperate and will not be creative. This is the end result of a leadership based on fear, and its side effects go even deeper and further.

If we want to know how to avoid future defeats, we must understand how the past ones occurred. According to the Arab philosopher, Ibn Khaldoun, "If the leader is an oppressive tyrant who uses punishment to impose himself and searches for people's mistakes, they become afraid and humiliated, and use lies, deceit and cunning to escape his wrath. They consequently adopt this sort of behaviour, and develop corrupt insights and low morale, and they will probably abandon him when he is in dire straits and in war."[1]

We are not interested in counting mistakes but in counting achievements. We are not searching for candidates to criticize but to praise, not to frustrate but to motivate, and not to punish but to reward. We forgive and forget mistakes but we always remember good and successful actions.

So we call upon our youth to produce, create and make mistakes. This is where our leadership has led us today. The era when an official's absence caused confusion is gone forever. Today we have a large team of qualified young men and women, any one of whom can single-handedly manage a major project and succeed.

How did we achieve this? By accommodating some mistakes, training and encouraging people, delegating power, following up and monitoring. Not all mistakes are the same. We all commit mistakes and learn from them. The leader must forgive unintentional mistakes, but should investigate those made out of negligence, procrastination and similar behaviour.

In my opinion, success and failure are not permanent. If someone failed twice in eight attempts I would still consider him successful, but would also want to analyze the failures. It is not enough to simply say that the person failed – we need to know why. Was it something personal, was it the fault of someone else or was it an error in the vision or in its implementation? Were there any lessons that could be learned from the failure and were there obstacles that can be removed to achieve success?

The famous Arab leader Salahuddin Al Ayoubi[2] once noted, "To make a mistake in clemency is better in my opinion than to be right in punishment." When young officials make mistakes, especially for the first time, the last thing a true leader should do is to punish them. If the leader does so, the officials will become afraid, isolate themselves and lack the confidence to do a good job in the future. The leader should rather give these officials the opportunity to redress and correct their mistakes. He must not rush to punish them, but rather help them learn from their mistakes and teach them to use their mistakes as springboards to the right action.

Some people confuse decisiveness with harshness. It is not harshness if a parent acts decisively with a child, because the parent's ultimate goal is to help them avoid future mistakes and succeed. When I think about my late father, I remember a relationship that combined love with respect. I respected him because he was the leader, but would still have respected otherwise because he was my father.

A subordinate must know that a leader is always there to help and support him. It is only natural for a manager to take an interest in a dynamic, creative employee, but he should also realize that not all employees have the same strengths.

Love and respect crown my strong bonds with HH Sheikh Khalifa bin Zayed Al Nahyan, President of the UAE and Ruler of Abu Dhabi.

The late Sheikh Zayed and Sheikh Rashid inspired me in leadership.

Sheikh Zayed was like a guiding father to me.

In conversation with Sheikh Zayed bin Sultan, Founder of the UAE.

Our initiatives complement the achievements of my father, Sheikh Rashid.

With my brothers, the late Sheikh Maktoum and Sheikh Hamdan.

With the Crown Prince of Abu Dhabi, HH Sheikh Mohammed bin Zayed bin Sultan Al Nahyan.

LEFT: Visiting UAE troops participating at the UN-led peacekeeping mission in Kosovo, with Sheikh Mohammed bin Zayed.

Meeting Queen Elizabeth II.

With US Secretary of State Hillary Clinton.

Receiving South Korean President Lee Myung-bak.

With Turkish Prime Minister Recep Tayyip Erdoğan.

With Victoria, Crown Princess of Sweden and Duchess of Västergötland.

Meeting UN Secretary-General Ban Ki-moon.

Receiving Prime Minister of India Dr Manmohan Singh.

With former Prime Minister of Spain José Luis Rodríguez Zapatero.

Delivering the inaugural annual report for the UAE Office for the Coordination of Foreign Aid.

Addressing the Summit on the Global Agenda in Dubai.

Speaking at the opening of the Federal National Council.

Attending the Arab Summit in Khartoum, Sudan.

Meeting King Abdullah bin Abdulaziz of Saudi Arabia.

With Sheikh Hamad bin Khalifa Al Thani, Emir of Qatar.

With King Abdullah II of Jordan.

With President of Algeria Abdelaziz Bouteflika.

With King Hamad bin Isa Al Khalifa of Bahrain.

With Sultan Qaboos bin Said of Oman.

With King Mohammed VI of Morocco.

With Sheikh Sabah Al Ahmad Al Sabah, Emir of Kuwait.

With HH Sheikh Khalifa bin Zayed Al Nahyan and Members of the Supreme Council Rulers of the Emirates.

During a UAE cabinet meeting.

With HH Sheikh Khalifa and Members of the Supreme Council Rulers of the Emirates, commemorating the UAE National Day at the Union House in Dubai.

A leader must afford his people the opportunity to correct their mistakes, improve their performance and establish a balanced relationship with him. Only then will young officials strive to avoid mistakes because they do not want to disappoint their leader and not because they are afraid of being punished. With such officials, we could end up with a team capable of conquering any obstacle.

What you give your subordinates, they will give you in return. Hold them in high esteem and they will appreciate you; love them and they will love you; support them and they will support you; lead them from the front and they will follow you to the end of the world. Is this a secret formula or a puzzle? Could anything be simpler?

The racer and the race

A civil servant once visited me at the diwan[3] and humbly thanked me for promoting him to the position of deputy director of a government department, adding that he hoped he would live up to my expectations. When the man asked permission to leave, I held his hand, asked him to sit down and said, "Mohammed, do not think that your promotion was a coincidence. I have been monitoring your performance for four years and know everything about you." The man looked startled. "Me? I am nobody," he exclaimed, "there are tens of thousands of civil servants like me!"

"You were until something happened that made us take an interest in you and monitor your performance."

The man seemed even more amazed, so I called for a young man named Moadhed, a member of the 'secret shoppers' team, and asked him to tell the audience the story of that civil servant. Mohammed would never sit in his office for long periods of time and often went to the trading floor. On one occasion, he helped an old investor complete his formalities, offered him tea and accompanied him to the door. He would help other people in a similar way, going beyond the call of duty. One of the people he helped was Moadhed, who later submitted a report about Mohammed's professional behaviour and competence.

When, after four years, I heard that Mohammed had resigned his job to join a better-paying job in the private sector, I decided to make a more tempting offer and promote him to deputy director of his department. The decision did not only surprise him, but also surprised his boss and all the employees in that department.

I like surprises and bringing people good news that promises them better status and success. I wish I could announce a new and unique project every day of my life – the kind of project that needs exemplary people whom I can count on. I might sometimes appear more firm than necessary with some senior managers, although deep in my heart, I have nothing more than gratitude and esteem for their achievements. Whatever the project, the response has always been excellent.

In an age of constant change, our needs and requirements are always evolving. Our projects expand, become more complex and require new blood to achieve their goals. Some people think I want to engage the maximum number of participants possible in the race for excellence and present me with long lists of prospects, but does not match the workings of my vision.

The only thing that could ever guarantee success is to have the largest number of *excellent* achievers on board, because the race for excellence calls for exceptional participants. The tools for creativity are available in the market and we can buy them whenever we want to, whether from the United States, Japan, Europe or elsewhere. But creativity itself is not a product we can buy and nor is enthusiasm. We have to look for those who have these characteristics and nurture their talents.

Protocol calls for the leader to meet with the director of a department behind closed doors and discuss the department's affairs. This is not my way of doing things. Any experienced observer can spot a dynamic employee who takes initiative and develops the system, in every department or company. We want an open door policy in place, one that will lead us to such achievers – dedicated people who would otherwise work silently, like unknown soldiers.

No matter how excellent any director is, we still need to cultivate talented and promising achievers from the third and fourth level of management. They are the natural reserves we need; the store of creative human resources needed to pioneer the future, but only after nurturing their talents and providing them with the appropriate training and experience.

This is not a haphazard process and will not result from spontaneous action, coincidence or whim. A creative person might lose inspiration after two years for some reason; a nonperformer might see the light and become an achiever for another.

Monitoring the performance of those who are not in the frontline is therefore a delicate matter that calls for a methodical approach. Lists of skills and potential should be drawn up. Candidates on List A, for example, might be capable of managing departments within a short span of time; List B candidates might need two years before they are ready for the task. Other lists would include those fit to lead a team, those qualified to be members of a team and those whose performances still need monitoring.

Nurturing creativity

Bureaucrats are self-declared enemies of change. There is nothing like bureaucracy to kill creativity and simple, efficient problem-solving. I do not like bureaucracy and bureaucrats; I prefer the company of creative people who lead at work, fulfil their obligations and improve performance and productivity, then follow them up. These are the people we can rely upon.

Such people are the focus of my interest and care. This does not mean that I do not trust those in senior positions. But the fact is that people are a leader's true wealth, and the leader should maintain that wealth and focus on organizing human resources. This is a country's most important investment and just like any other major investment, it needs ample research and dedicated follow-up.

I may know all about the head of the managerial structure, but I always want to know about the pillars that are supporting that structure. It is only normal for open governments to make all their departments accessible to people, so that they are aware of the department's functions and can make suggestions to improve their systems.

I want to tap the potential of people, inspire them to generate great ideas, help them develop wealth, and transform their ideas into major projects and job opportunities.

We can do this, not only in the UAE, but in the whole Arab world. This is not just an important quest, but a sacred mission entrusted to me, to civil servants and to every official in the Arab world. Nothing is more important than people. When journalists ask me what the budget is for a specific project, I always say that the budget is available but that our biggest budget is for those talented young men and women who we rely on to implement our projects.

Most company managers spend a substantial part of their time searching for suitable talent to fill available vacancies. I, on the other hand, spend a substantial part of my time searching for the right positions for talented people. We have a large number of qualified people who have made us very proud, and we have the right number of projects to employ qualified university graduates. But what we really need to do is to coach and nurture our gifted and creative young people and contribute to the realization of their ideas and dreams by transforming their ideas into successful businesses. Such businesses, in turn, would employ other young graduates. This would promote better interaction between the public and private sectors, and pave the way to generating a new breed of businessmen capable of undertaking remarkable ventures.

One of our initiatives that aims to achieve this is the Mohammed bin Rashid Establishment for Young Business Leaders,[4] the first venture undertaken by the Dubai Development and Investment Authority. The new corporation was launched simultaneously with an Islamic

Development Fund in 2002. The fund, capitalized at AED 700 million, was instated with the collaboration of the Dubai Islamic Bank.

Known in short as 'Riyadah' (pioneering), the corporation aims at coaching hundreds of young business people and providing their ventures with guaranteed marketing channels. The public and private sectors are compelled by law to purchase at least 5 per cent of their requirements from these new ventures which, in return, must guarantee their products and services are competitive and up to the highest international standards.

The other advantages provided by the organization include:

- Providing finance through a development fund
- Providing finance with preferential terms
- Financing up to 90 per cent of the cost of new ventures
- Providing easy terms on loans, starting from the second year of marketing the project's products

Women

Wherever I have mentioned young people in this book, I was, of course, referring to both the UAE's young men and women. I have, however, some remarks I would now like to add about our young women.

Some time ago, a US media delegation toured Dubai Internet City while on their first visit to the region. Since many people in the 'knowledge age' do not have the slightest idea about Dubai, or may have been misled by biased or incomplete information, the members of that delegation asked whether women were allowed to work at DIC. They were surprised to learn that 52 per cent of the people working there were women.

I was also astonished at that figure, but for very different reasons. We have a peculiar situation in the UAE, where there are more female students attending our universities than there are male students. A large number of our young men travel to study overseas or find employment at a comparatively young age, with the result that three quarters of the graduates at our local universities are young women. This is why I was astonished at the percentage – I thought it would be much higher.

Over the next ten years, we will need the talent of all our university graduates. The percentage of female graduates taking up jobs generated by the expansion of present projects and the launch of new ones will become even higher. Since I consider this situation normal, I see no reason to change it. I also do not see any reason to impose 'positive discrimination' in favour of employing more men in the future and in fact, have never seen this as necessary.

When I was inspecting a government department some time ago, the director told me that the number of women in its labour force was approaching 70 per cent and that he consequently had to ask the department's personnel manager, a woman herself, to temporarily halt hiring women in favour of men. Since the director of that department did not want anyone to get the wrong impression without knowing the reason behind this action, he explained the situation to me, in case I received any protest. Although I actually received no complaint in this regard, my position in such situations is well known.

"Is the performance of any of the women employed by your department unsatisfactory?" I asked.

"No," he responded. "The qualifications of all the women applying to join this department meet our requirements or are even higher."

"Then employ all the women who successfully pass the department's test and meet its requirements," I said, "and keep hiring them even if the percentage of female employees reaches 100".

Employment standards call for comparing competency, academic qualifications, experience, capabilities and openness to development; not gender, colour or social status. This is not only the civilized way of dealing with employment, it is also the right way to deal with people in both the public and private sectors, and reach social justice in modern communities.

The second thing that amazes me is the fact that there are not more women leaders in our society. Women have a special status in our society and should therefore occupy a more prominent position. They deserve to be honoured and occupy the positions they have earned. We have very capable ladies in leading positions and I expect our leaders to keep the momentum and appoint the right staff to leading positions, regardless of gender and according to their qualifications, efficiency and enthusiasm. The initiative of launching the female leaders qualification programme is just the first of what I hope will be a succession of programmes aimed at empowering women to take on senior managerial positions within a few years. This will put women on par with men and make them full partners in work and success. It is the duty of leaders to discover and nurture female leadership talent and coach them until they can assume senior managerial roles, even if it threatens their own jobs.

There is nothing women lack to prevent them from becoming leaders. History is full of female leaders who played a crucial role in advancing the cause of civilization, developing their communities and promoting creativity. I believe that Emirati women can do much more than they are presently doing to serve our nation – provided they are given the right encouragement and empowerment.

Our experience in granting women equal job opportunities in the UAE has proven to be one of the most successful in the Arab world. Emirati women are now involved in prestigious projects in all fields, including engineering, science, technology, management and computer programming. I believe that the interest the UAE government has taken in advancing and empowering women is unequalled in the Arab world.

Today, Emirati women can work wherever they please, establish their own companies, and do not face the kind of restrictions limiting some of their Arab counterparts elsewhere. The willingness of women to work in an environment that preserves and respects their dignity and professionalism, and their subsequent success in their chosen careers, has contributed to overcoming many of the social obstacles restricting their work in the past. This has happened relatively quickly and in a calm, wise and positive manner. In this regard, we have successfully overcome the sensitivities and complications that exist in a number of other societies.

I regularly meet with businesswomen, teachers and all other sorts of working women, in order to get acquainted with their opinions on a variety of topics. I feel that working women are eager to prove themselves, their capabilities, experience and performance, not only on a local level but also on an international level. Women, in general, deal with their jobs more tactfully and are more deeply committed to their work. As a result of the continuous motivation, encouragement and enabling programmes, we see more women in leading positions and women employees awarded in the Dubai Government Excellence Program.

What we have achieved so far is considerable and I believe that the near future will bring even more developments that will further encourage optimism and determination in women. That is why I have always encouraged them to join the labour market, establish companies, launch new ventures, enter the vocations that suit them most and focus on upgrading their professional skills.

All women, not just those in senior positions, should try to achieve such goals. We must excel regardless of the type of work we do, because excellence is the only way to realize our goals and ambitions.

The idea factory

Our minds are factories of ideas – the higher the quality of the raw material we absorb, the better the quality of the final product. We know that we still have a long way to go, but we always insist on providing our young people with the highest possible quality of assistance to help them prepare for the future and develop their initiative, along with their creative, pioneering spirit.

Leaders carry heavy burdens. They should set examples, generate visions, take decisions, but he or she is not the only one endowed with a pioneering mind.Development is a collaborative effort and contributing to it is not only done through work, but also involves an elaborate thought process. A leader is not, therefore, required to generate all the ideas needed and all those who can contribute to this process should do so.

The person with the best idea is not always the best one to present it, and must consequently present it to others who can possibly add some aspects and improve it. A successful leader is not one who insists that his ideas are the best and the only ones that deserve to be implemented; he is one who encourages others to develop and present new ideas.

When presented with a promising idea, a wise leader should ask the person who conceived it to submit a feasibility study. When convinced about the project's feasibility, the leader should approve the idea and authorize its implementation, while undertaking to provide all the support necessary to make it a success.

When a leader involves all those capable of generating good ideas, he makes them partners in leading the development process. When this happens, we are no longer talking about a manager and a subordinate, or a leader and a follower, but about a leadership team that develops, takes initiatives, implements and allows us to outpace others by a large extent.

While it is true that human creativity, vision, patriotism, defence of our citizens' interests and achievements, and promotion of national identity are the essential ingredients in building a modern and competitive state, our strategic goals require a different sort of effort.

Some leadership traits that were useful in the past might not be so today, because we are facing a situation that is totally different from the one that prevailed in the late 1990s or even in the early 2000s. We must therefore find new forms of leadership, because the sophisticated ventures we are considering today require a higher level of initiative and creativity.

These are mega projects requiring the largest number of creative people – those who are highly skilled in development and improvizing solutions – that we can get our hands on. We cannot meet those requirements by solely relying on half of our society. Everybody must take part and upgrade their skills. Those who do not will have no place of importance in these projects, because they will not be able to compete. This is the challenge our young men and women must face and overcome.

This challenge should not, however, hide the more important situation that will face our society in the future. Today, we are working for tomorrow and in the future, young people will be working for their future. But if jobs, wealth and projects are easily available, and everything is perfectly in place, there will be no challenge left for our youth.

Those who think we are aiming to provide future generations with all sorts of amenities so that they can enjoy a luxurious and complacent lifestyle, do not understand our development goals.

While it is true that we are building new cities, constructing roads, manufacturing, establishing companies and realizing projects, our ultimate goal is to develop minds so that they can master how to successfully deal with the challenges of the future. If we cannot do this, our development will have lost track of our vision and at that time, we cannot ask the students to take the blame for the mistakes of their teachers.

If, in the future, young people find good opportunities, let them exploit them successfully and allow all members of society to benefit from them. If they cannot find such opportunities, they must be ready to make them. They must harvest fruit from the sand, tap water from the desert and render the soil fertile as we have done. The Prophet (PBUH) once said, "Whoever revives a barren land will be rewarded, and the effort he made in doing so will be accredited to his favour as charity whenever any creature benefits from it."[5]

They must do all this and more, and be prepared to realize grand schemes from scratch. If some of our young people think this mission is impossible, I would like them to open their windows and take a look around them... then I will tell them, "Nearly all of what you see before you was created from nothing. There was nothing before but the sand of the desert."

---

1 Ibn Khaldoun, *The Muqaddimah of Ibn Khaldoun*, Beirut: Al Hilal, p. 101.

2 Salahuddin Al Ayoubi, also known as Salah Ad-Din Yusuf Ibn Ayyub (1137/1138–1193), became the first Sultan of Egypt and Syria, and founded the Ayyubid dynasty. His army defeated the Crusaders at the Battle of Hattin, leading to his recapture of Palestine, which had been seized from the Fatimid Egyptians by the Crusaders eighty-eight years earlier. At the height of his power, his sultanate included Egypt, Syria, Mesopotamia, Hejaz, Yemen, and parts of North Africa.

3 The ruler's office.

4 Mohammed bin Rashid Establishment for Young Business Leaders was established in 2002, and is concerned with the development and growth of the small and medium business sector.

5 *Musnad Ahmad Ibn Hanbal*, narrated by Ahmad bin Mohammed bin Hanbal; and *Sunan Al Nisai*, narrated by Ahmad Ibn Shu'ayb Al Nasai and freely translated from the Arabic.

CHAPTER EIGHT

The Importance of My Horses

A horse trainer once asked me to allow one of my horses to run in a race. I asked him to choose another horse because I was sure the horse he favoured was ill. The trainer was astonished. He said he knew the horse very well and that veterinary doctors had, in any case, examined him and given him the 'all clear'. He insisted the horse be given the chance to take part and was sure it would win.

Although I tried to explain that no one knows my horses better than I do, he left unconvinced and after some time, our difference of opinion became public. I decided to settle the matter and sought the opinion of international experts who examined the horse. Their report showed the horse had two small fractured bones in his neck.

Many people asked how I knew this, and some even suggested I had a special gift in understanding horses, but the answer was very simple.

Is it not normal that a parent knows when his child is suffering from some illness? And is it not also normal that a leader knows when there is a problem, by just taking a look at the head of a work team or one of its members?

A foreign journalist once asked me what I would learned during twenty-five years of breeding horses and racing them in Europe. I told her that I had not learned anything I did not already know in Dubai.

The journalist was amazed. "Were not all those consultants, experts and trainers useful in any respect?"

"When I started racing my horses in Europe, everybody advised me to surround myself with experts, so that they could accompany me if I wanted to buy or sell horses or participate in a race," I responded. "I surrounded myself with the best in the industry, but my horses never reached the top until I started managing them myself, taking care of their food, health and training."

The journalist looked perplexed. "How did you manage this without any expert help or advice?"

"The reason I succeeded where they failed was because the consultants, experts and trainers had bogged themselves down in such minute detail, that they failed to see when a horse was only standing on three legs!"

Such people think the same way, not only when it comes to horses, but in nearly everything else they do. So if anyone asks me how Dubai achieved so much at such record speed, I will simply say that it is because we never drowned ourselves in excessive detail. The key to a true and effective development process is a vision that does not allow small details to cloud its basic goals.

We are development oriented people, brought up on the love of horses and the desert ever since we were infants, and therefore we know how to discipline our horses and we understand the desert winds. It is a knowledge we accumulated over time.

A foreign journalist once asked me to name the best jockey. I hesitated for some time, because if I told her it was Willie Carson,[1] Frankie Dettori[2] or any other famous jockey, the other jockeys would feel insulted, especially coming from the world's largest racehorse owner. So I told her that it was me.

The journalist continued, asking, "If you are really the best jockey, how come you do not appear in our races?"

"I take part in 160-kilometre endurance races – your races are too short for me."

Before the interview was over, the journalist asked me to name my favourite course. By now I had an uneasy feeling she was trying to put me on the spot. If I had said it was Ascot,[3] Newmarket[4] or York,[5] the managers of the other excellent courses would have felt insulted, so I said, "The course that is a descent for my horses and an ascent for others."

I do not find it strange when foreign journalists tell me that my answers amaze them, even though they are spontaneous. But I do find it somewhat strange when Arab journalists ask me why I take such an interest in horses.

"My brother, you are an Arab just like me," I tell them. "You read the Holy Qur'an, the words of the Prophet (PBUH) and the story of his life, so why do you ask me such a question? Horses are not just like other animals. They bless the house of their owner, are the pride of every Arab and a symbol of strength, magnanimity and power. Did you not read what God said in his Holy Book? "Against them, prepare your strength to the utmost of your power, including steeds of war, to strike terror in the hearts of the enemies."[6] The Prophet (PBUH) said, "Blessings are tied to the forelocks of horses till Judgement Day."[7]

The Prophet (PBUH) Himself was very keen on horses and they are often mentioned in hadiths. In one, Jarir (May God bless him) reported, "The Prophet (PBUH) never curtailed me ever since I converted to Islam, and never met me without smiling at me. When I once complained to him that I could not sit still on a horse, he banged his hand on my chest and said, 'Please God, enable him to sit firmly and guide him and enlighten him."[8]

When I participate in endurance races and encourage my sons and daughters to race, and when I enjoy horses and inspire my children to enjoy them, I am doing something our religion encourages. That is why I wonder, when Arab journalists ask me why I race, if they have ignored the fact that the Prophet (PBUH) used to organize horse races.

In his book of corroborated words of the Prophet (PBUH), Al Bukhari reported, "Ibn Omar (May God bless them) had said the Prophet (PBUH) organized a race between *mudammarah* horses[9] from the al-Hafia area to the Thaniat al-Wadae area, which was the longest racecourse at the time. When I asked Musa how long it was, he said that it ranged between six and seven miles. He also told me that the Prophet (PBUH) organized a race between normal horses from Thaniat al-Wadae to the Bani Zureiq Mosque. When I asked him about the length of that course, he said it was about one mile long, and that Ibn Omar took part to it."[10]

Some of us may have forgotten that our Arab nation was once a pioneering nation and mastered the use of horses. I will never forget this. I spoke about the pioneering spirit in a previous chapter of this book and I would like to add here that all nations like horses, the difference being that we Arabs do not only like them, we also respect and honour them, and consider them good omens. The book *Tafsir Al Manam*, which explains dreams, says that if a pregnant woman dreams of a mare, this is a good omen, telling her that she will have a baby boy; and if an unmarried woman dreams of a mare, this means that she will be married to a good man.

All nations are keen on their horses and take good care of them, but Arabs made horses and their ancestries a science. More than 1,000 years ago many Arabs wrote books about horses.

Arab poets also specialized in describing the special features of unique horses. The most famous poems were those of renowned poets such as Umru'lqais,[11] Al Mutanabbi[12] and Antarah.[13]

When I imagine Arab knights and military leaders, I see them riding their horses, leading armies all around the world, and writing wonderful poems that speak of great ideas and valour. But the time of such great exploits and glorious days is over.

Arabian horses no longer carry great knights and leaders, but when the sun was setting on the pioneering exploits of the Arabs and their mastery of horses, it was rising in the West on their horses of Arab origin. It is known that all thoroughbreds in England are the descendants of Arabian horses, the world's oldest horse ancestry. This was done either through direct imports or by cross-breeding three famous stallions: Byerly Turk, Godolphin Barb or Godolphin Arabian (referring to a horse of Moroccan origin, bred from Arabian horses and used to conquer Andalusia) and Darley Arabian.

Most people do not know that an Arab symbol was present in the decisive Battle of Waterloo, where the Duke of Wellington defeated Napoleon Bonaparte in 1815. Napoleon was riding the white Arabian thoroughbred Marengo, while the Duke of Wellington was riding Copenhagen, a descendent of the Arabian thoroughbred Darley Arabian.

Poetry, chivalry, pedigree, magnanimity, prestige and generosity are the established values of Arab chivalry, but the past is the past. When the Arab knight disappeared, his horse remained... and for a while, even the Arab horse was on the verge of extinction. If we leave economy, technology, pioneering and horses to others, what will be left for us?

I believe that those who do not understand the reason behind our keen interest in horses will not understand what we are trying to do. We want to regain our pioneering status – and not only in economy, technology and excellence.

We now have superb breeding stables and racecourses in Dubai and elsewhere in the United Arab Emirates. In Europe and other major centres, our horses and jockeys are racing in international events, winning the world's most prestigious races and collecting all sorts of trophies and prizes. I cannot claim that we have totally regained our past pioneering status in horsemanship, but I can say – if you will excuse the pun – that we are on the right track.

E-government, which Dubai initiated in the Arab world, has now gained ground in several Arab countries. Dubai no longer monopolizes shopping festivals, because many Arab cities are now hosting similar events. Our expertise in managing free zones, ports and airports has become a fully fledged training ground. We consider it our duty to share this expertise with neighbouring countries, just as we are sharing our expertise in breeding and racing horses.

Races that are currently being organized in Egypt, Jordan, Syria, Spain and other countries, play a crucial role in reviving interest in horse breeding and trade. Many people are now dusting off ancient manuscripts dealing with traditional methods of breeding and caring for this unique animal.

Whoever thinks that we are interested only in the economic aspect of breeding and racing horses is wrong, because our love of horses runs like the blood in our veins. Horsemanship is an activity and sport for the body and the soul. It is one of the most important sources in generating positive energy in human beings.

This, however, does not discount the economic aspect of breeding and racing horses, which is certainly a big industry in the West. The races that we participate in overseas are becoming profitable and breeding horses is providing thousands of jobs all around the world. Given enough time and interest, the same can happen in the Arab world, which thousands of years ago, was, after all, the most important birthplace of horses on earth.

In the *Lisan al-Arab* (the language of the Arabs),[14] politics is defined as managing by reforming, developing and enhancing; so a ruler manages his people by reforming and developing, as the horse trainer manages the horses by grooming and taming. This means that politics is the act of a manager regardless of what he is managing. That explains why people were fascinated with horses throughout history – they saw some human traits in them, so they domesticated them, trained them and learned from them.

My fascination with horses is not only because I am a poet, but because I love and understand them. If your admiration and love for horses is limited to their beautiful physical appearance, then you do not know much about horses, because you fail to see their inner beauty. You will not learn how to deal properly with horses until you see beyond their physical appearance; only then will you appreciate and understand the Arabian horse, and the horse in return will appreciate and understand you. That is why in Arabic we say, "horses know a real rider" and vice versa. Early Arabic poems reflect that poets did not think of their horses as animals, but rather as human beings and friends.

Not every rider is a horseman and not every horseman is a knight. A horseman is one who rides a horse, but a knight is a horseman who knows the meaning of riding his horse. It is chivalry, magnanimity and pedigree; that is why I am proud that I understand horses.

The back of a horse is not just a saddle, but a place where a knight is elevated to unique heights – the kind of feeling that opens horizons for conceiving visions and new ideas. It is the kind of feeling that frees the mind from the monotony of daily affairs and allows a leader to see the road ahead. Only then does he know the right direction to follow, the goals he wants to achieve and the prospects for both him and his people.

Whenever I am with my horses, you will see me scurrying between them, wiping the sweat from one and taking the pulse of another, feeding them, training them and teaching them everything that will ennoble them. This kind of relationship is, however not one-sided, as I not only teach them but also learn from them. I learn from people around me and from my horses. Whoever knows how to love and respect a horse will also know how to treat people with equal love and respect; and whoever knows how to raise the morale of horses also knows how to lift the spirits of those around him. What you give them they will give you in return and if you encourage them, they will overcome difficulties and take you to victory.

---

1 Willie Carson or William Fisher Hunter Carson (born 1942) is a retired jockey in thoroughbred horse racing.
2 Frankie Dettori or Lanfranco "Frankie" Dettori (born 1970) is an Italian horse racing jockey.
3 A famous English racecourse, located in the small town of Ascot, Berkshire.
4 A legendary racecourse located in Newmarket, Suffolk, England. It is the headquarters of British horse racing, and home to the largest cluster of training yards in the country, as well as many key horse racing organizations.
5 A horse racing track in the southwest of the city of York in North Yorkshire, England.
6 Sura Al Anfal, v. 26.
7 *Sahih Bukhari*, narrated by Mohammed Ibn Ismail Al Bukhari and freely translated from the Arabic.
8 *Sahih Bukhari*, narrated by Mohammed Ibn Ismail Al Bukhari and freely translated from the Arabic.
9 Horses that have undergone a special diet and exercise regime to make them lean.
10 *Sahih Bukhari*, narrated by Mohammed Ibn Ismail Al Bukhari and freely translated from the Arabic.
11 Umru'lqais or Umru Al Qais bin Hujr Al Kindi was an Arabian poet in the sixth century AD, and also the son of one of the last Kindite kings. He is sometimes considered the father of Arabic poetry.
12 Al Mutanabbi or Abu At Tayyib Ahmad Ibn Al Husayn Al Mutanabbi (915–965) was originally from the Arabian peninsula but was born within the modern-day boundaries of Iraq, which was then part of the Abbasid caliphate. He is considered as one of the greatest poets in the Arabic language.
13 Antarah or Antarah Ibn Shaddad Al Absi was a pre-Islamic Arabian hero and poet (525–608) famous for both his poetry and his adventurous life. One of his best poems is contained in the *Mu'allaqat*. The account of his life forms the basis of a long and extravagant romance.
14 *Lisan al-Arab* (*The Arab Tongue*), narrated by Mohammad Ibn Mukarram Ibn Ali Ibn Ahmad Ibn Manzur and freely translated from the Arabic.

CHAPTER NINE

Positive and Negative Energy

During those rare times when I enjoy some moments of relaxation, if I am not riding horses, I am passionately watching them. Fourteen years ago, I noticed an amazing feature of this astonishing animal: if horses are fed the same food, trained in the same monotonous manner, are often shouted at and are not encouraged by their keepers, they will start to decline and lose their energy.

If that is the case with horses, what would happen to human beings if they are treated this way? When employees are unhappy with the prevailing situation at their workplace, such as the slow and monotonous pace of their work, or a lack of direction and quality management from their superiors, their morale will deteriorate, their work will suffer and their performance will decline. If the opposite is true, all will be fine.

Employees are usually frustrated because they feel insecure, are mistreated, given false promises, see their hopes dashed, suffer boring routine and poor support services and have to face repeated blame, bias and injustice. Some managers stifle the potential of their employees, prevent them from using their initiative and bully them. Others give their assistants free rein to treat employees harshly, therefore depriving them of all opportunities to show their talent and efficiency and consequently, from getting promoted.

Such behaviour is unacceptable because it leads to frustration, which is an illness just like all other illnesses. This is an illness that has a cure. Nevertheless, before prescribing any medicine, the manager must make sure that his managerial policy is not the reason for frustration.

How many managers have inhibited the potential of their employees and driven them to despair? How can we work without an adequately motivated workforce? How can we expect to regain our pioneering status and achieve our goals under such circumstances?

We can monitor a leader's performance through the morale of his team. Armies do not defeat their enemies because they have the right weapons and infrastructure; they win and lose wars because of their morale. If the morale of a team is high, they will respond to the vision of their leader, achieve his goals and follow his footsteps, but if it is low, the leader has only himself to blame.

Negative energy

Although we are at the beginning of a new millennium and exploring new ideas, some Arab governments still fail to give their people any cause for optimism. This leads their citizens to become pessimistic and as a natural consequence, the whole society becomes pessimistic.

The mission of any government should be to promote its people's creativity and to understand that continuous humiliation, degradation and criticism stifle creativity. How can people be creative when they are afraid or frustrated? When bureaucracy is rampant, corruption is widespread, equal opportunity simply does not exist and most jobs and promotions are obtained through powerful people – you have a situation that leaves people with no hope for the present or the future.

This environment produces a totally demoralized citizen who cannot achieve any of his goals; one who cannot even dream about a better future because he is afraid to face the bitter reality when he wakes up each morning.

You simply cannot kill the power of dreaming in young people and then ask them to be creative and to excel. If you kill the dream, you kill hope; and if you kill hope, what kind of life will be left for people to live? It is only normal for young people to feel pessimistic and frustrated when they become entrapped in such a situation. And since young people who do not own anything have nothing to lose, they lose interest in everything.

We must separate problems, try to understand the reasons behind each one and find solutions for them. When a situation becomes complicated, a leader would need extreme courage to disentangle the problems and solve each one individually.

When this is not possible, it becomes even more difficult to find a way out. I do not know of any magical solution to get out of this vicious cycle, but I do know how one remains inside the cycle: through more humiliation, destroying morale, adding more pain to the pain already inflicted by external factors and then surrendering to the negative energy.

Certain people in our societies behave in ways that are not always easy to understand. If life means positive energy, does not negative energy mean the opposite? If we are convinced that life is worth living, should not we throw all our positive energy into our lives and try to make something out of them?

I once heard a story about a beautiful rose garden with a single weed growing in it. Two people went into the garden to have a look at it. When the first person came out he was asked what he had seen. "I have seen the most beautiful roses you could ever wish to see," he responded. The second person was asked the same question. "I saw an ugly weed," was the reply.

There are those who look at life positively and see in it everything that is beautiful, and those who look at it negatively and see everything that is ugly and unpleasant. How can one person look at something and find it beautiful while another person looks at the same thing and finds it ugly? Maybe beauty and ugliness emanate from the onlooker and not the object being looked at?

All nations outside the Arab world appear to be proud of their achievements. I do not know of any nation other than those in the Arab world that criticizes itself so harshly. When you hear the negative way people talk about Arabs, you would think doomsday is nigh and that God has forsaken us. Arabs tend to say, "We are losers, we are nothing. Nobody cares about us. We have lost everything."

This belief has became so rooted in some of us that we even let it rule our lives. Some criticize themselves so harshly that they become their own worst enemies as well as enemies of their nation. These people become so frustrated and pessimistic, that they no longer see anything positive, and consider anyone who tells them the world is still full of hope and promise to be a revisionist.[1]

I disagree with this mode of thinking. I believe revisionists and reactionaries kill positive energy in people and spread their negative energy. They kill hope and revive despair, stifle creativity and promote bureaucracy. They want to deter development and slow down modernization. They want the community to revert to the old customs and practices that are unsuitable for this era. These people do this because they want to protect their own interests and not those of the larger public.

Some believe that obstructing a march is easier than keeping pace with it and that destroying all the beautiful homes surrounding their ugly ones is easier than refurbishing their own. Why? Because they want to protect themselves – and their jobs – and believe they cannot compete with others. But laziness cannot compete with activity, creativity with monotony, nor motivation with frustration. These cannot rival each other, let alone even exist together. One of each must overtake its counterpart and take its place – and this does not happen simply by coincidence or wishful thinking.

Change

The tasks of a successful leader include searching for competent managers and administrators to fulfil his vision and goals. This task is never properly complete if he does not search for them among his active, creative and positive-thinking employees – those who are also full of hope for life and the future – in his own department. It is also not complete before the leader searches for those in his team who are frustrated, bored and exhausted, tries to revive their interest and lift them from their despondency. A leader should also try to change the conditions that led to a lowering of morale and drove his people to pessimism and inactivity.

I used to find, at government departments and ministries, frustrated employees engulfed by routine, bogged down by negative energy and devoid of creativity and innovation. The only thing that drove these employees to work were the salaries they collected at the end of each month. Every morning, they would go to their offices and in the evening they would go back home, having achieved nothing, day after day, week after week, month after month.

These employees worked using the same methods and following the same killer routine, while their departmental heads may have been even lazier than them, and more absorbed by routine and boredom. In fact, calling them 'idle resources' would be a compliment, implying that such resources could be revived and properly utilized. This kind of situation can carry on for years, without any development in productivity, and the work of the departments or ministries concerned will not be affected by their presence or absence.

What really comforts a good leader is that there is a competent, younger generation of leaders of whom we can be proud, taking over those departments and ministries. But comfort alone is not the right emotion for a leader, because he should not allow negative people to remain trapped in lethargy, routine and bureaucracy. A leader should be eager to introduce change from the grass-root level and let things start afresh.

A wise man once said, "Wishes are mere daydreams and the fantasy of the deprived." Change does not come by wishful thinking and the leader who just sits and wishes for change is, without doubt, a failure. It is a fact of life and means adapting yourself to the environment, because those who cannot adapt, cannot survive or coexist with their societies. If we agree that the world is going through change, we must also agree about the need for us to change in order to adapt.

In today's world, change is the rule and stagnation is the exception, because the latter equates to withdrawal and highlights the absence of competition. We want globalization to promote the competitive spirit. There are no other options – the world is changing and we must change with it. This conviction helps relieve the pains of change and reduce some of its side effects.

When we are convinced of the need to change, we can determine our pace towards change and choose our priorities. If we are not convinced, the world will impose change on us and we will be left with no options. Worse still, if we do not choose our own pace of change, the world will dictate it for us.

Our age requires everyone to be Internet-literate, so that no leader can hide his ignorance by prohibiting people to use the World Wide Web. He should rather learn to keep pace with the latest developments in economy and management, study the experiences of other nations, identify good opportunities and find the best ways to avail his country of them, and incorporate all of this in his vision.

We have discussed achievements and success extensively in this book and know by now that luck alone never led us to any of our achievements. Everything we have accomplished to date has been the fruit of concentrating our efforts on our goals and this will not change in the future. Therefore, anyone who discounts the importance of obstacles along the way and believes that he or she can sail to their destination, powered only by the favourable winds of conviction, is mistaken.

We must expect resistance to change, and therefore be prepared to convince reactionaries that their fears are groundless, and that our interests lie in introducing change.

If we expect the public sector to respond easily and immediately to proposed development plans, then we do not entirely understand the structure and legacy of our government departments. The negative impression people from all over the world have about government departments in general did not come from nowhere, but was rather the result of accumulated experience.

Whoever believes he can propose an action plan aimed at achieving excellence in the public sector and expects to hear the management shouting, "Let us go for it!" simply does not know these institutions. The word 'bureaucracy' is relatively new, but bureaucracy itself is a state of affairs that has accompanied mankind since the dawn of civilization. Traditionally, it is rather rare to find the public sector praised for its efficiency and productivity.

We also cannot expect that everybody, without exception, will embrace positive change, open closed doors, remove bottlenecks and facilitate people's business. Some managers by nature are unenthusiastic about change. Whenever you ask such managers to give up their rigid behaviour and obsolete practices to start showing the public some respect and real care, and to delegate some of their powers, it is only normal that they will find this difficult to comprehend and apply.

This type of change can become less difficult for employees to adopt when they find the right example in their leader. If the leader is not enthusiastic about change, he must not expect others to be. A leader who sincerely wants to introduce change must start by embracing it before asking others to do the same. Many leaders have tried to eradicate bureaucracy in their countries, only to find bureaucracy as firmly entrenched as ever when they stepped down. This does not prove the invincibility of bureaucracy, but simply shows how leaders have failed.

A leader must search for the reasons that some people resist change. When people are accustomed to a certain system they feel comfortable and secure with it. Change for such people means having to adapt to new realities, which some do not find easy, and they consequently stall and grab the first opportunity to refuse.

Refusal, however, does not mean something as radical as organizing demonstrations or strikes and could come in more subtle forms – such as someone saying 'yes' when they mean 'no'. Refusal does not mean refusing to work, but that production will be reduced to near zero. Those whose thinking and behaviour have been overtaken by negativity can delay and obstruct practically anything, hiding behind rules and procedures and faking ignorance.

In short, any person can behave negatively throughout the day, ensuring that no one else notices it. This can reach a point where some of those who do not know the reality may even consider this person to be a good employee, simply by what they see.

Some leaders use the powers vested in them to forcibly impose change – a 'whether-you-like-it-or-not' kind of approach. Others may even use outright force. Here in Dubai, we do not act this way and have opted for a civilized approach, because we believe it is the best way to deal with the citizens of our country. Although building is more difficult than destroying, peace more difficult than war and convincing more difficult than imposing, these three ways are more enduring.

We want everybody to cooperate, out of the conviction that whatever change we introduce is in the interest of the public. I cannot find a better way to reach this understanding than by convincing each and every one of our citizens. We have negative and positive powers, laziness and dynamism, creativity and stagnation, and fear and peace of mind. All our fears of change are nothing more than illusions and we must assure those who are afraid of change that it generates long-term job opportunities and does not reduce them.

We must also tell them how change will bring a rise in productivity, promote the position of employees instead of weakening it, and how taking care of the public will drive them to respect employees and appreciate their efforts. We must remove fear and maintain a sense of security, awaken creativity and eliminate laziness, and focus on positive energy and reject negativity. We must convince people of the right way forward time and time again, using all the positive methods available to us.

If we are armed with powerful arguments and determination, we will be able to convince people – at least most of them – of the benefits of change. Once convinced, people will start embracing change; and when this happens, they will start discovering positive aspects they never knew existed in their work. They will hear people sincerely thanking them and will find great pleasure in serving people. They will soon discover they can develop their work, increase productivity, offer useful suggestions, contribute to the development of their respective departments and enjoy the feeling of achievement and accomplishment.

If the reader concludes from what I have written that negative energy only exists in the public sector and that the private sector is immune to it, then this is not what I meant.

A journalist once told me, "You say that the mission of the public sector is to facilitate the performance of the private sector, but some people in the latter do not see things this way."

"I cannot blame them," I replied. "Today's economy incorporates modern and traditional trade. Those dealing in traditional trade are finding it difficult to convert to modern methods and want to retain their old ways. The private sector is dynamic by nature. The new generation of businessmen understands the requirements of dealing with the modern economy and has not faced the same difficulties the old generation had to endure while adapting to it."

Leaders and leadership

We in the United Arab Emirates have been blessed by a leadership that has faith in God and its people and wants the people of the UAE to prosper and develop. It does not want the younger generation to simply dream about their future but would like to help them fulfil their dreams. Our youth does not suffer from the problems of other Arab countries, so why should we feel pessimistic about their future? We have achieved a lot, so why are we focusing on what we have not achieved? Is this not a negative attitude? Are we not like the person who focused on just one weed and did not see the glorious roses surrounding it?

Think positively and you will see things positively. Our country is doing well and God willing, will continue to do so. We have achieved a lot and a lot more is coming, so let us be optimistic and spread positive attitudes throughout our society. This cannot be achieved by words, but through work, ventures, success stories and by allocating specific responsibilities to people and allowing them to become productive.

If jobs are not available, we cannot exploit the potential of our country – a potential that lies in the minds of our youth and in their confidence in themselves and in their country.

Motivation fuels excellence in people and stirs their positive energy. It is the power that sparks action, initiative, loyalty and creativity. It is also the basis of success and the key to achieving goals. The most successful leader must then, by definition, be the one most capable of motivating his people. He is the one most capable of encouraging them to create and excel. There is no doubt that motivation and high morale drives the performance of the employee to the peak.

I am committed to the promise I have given all our talented, hardworking and qualified young citizens, even those in secondary and tertiary managerial posts, of the chance to reach leadership positions when they deserve it. I wish that all the UAE's youth could become leaders, but unfortunately, not all of them qualify at this level. Our younger generation has matured enough to understand this. They also understand that excellence is not restricted to leaders and that positions are not always a precise measure of efficiency.

Salaries, on the other hand, should be linked to productivity and the level of achievement should set the level of material reward. Promotions may be regular or exceptional and sometimes, very exceptional. Although we have a rewards-and-motivation system, we must always encourage people in other, non-financial ways. This motivates people to excel, develop and achieve, while avoiding routine.

When an employee feels that his superior is monitoring his performance and shows his appreciation verbally and in writing, his morale will remain high and he will know that responding to this encouragement is his way to excellence and achievement as well as promotion and financial benefits. This will assure him that his advancement depends on his own performance and that the rest is only a matter of time.

All of the above are necessary tools and behaviour to encourage employees to produce, develop and excel. Nothing is better than an achievement to motivate a person to perform further. Financial and moral incentives are important, and it is equally important to provide a working environment that promotes excellence. An employee should be proud of his work and achievement is the key to pride.

Achievement is the crowning glory of an endeavour and not its starting point. It is also evidence that when channeled properly, potential and expertise will certainly lead to achievement. These are the elements that must be provided for the younger generation before they can really succeed: excellent training, an appropriate working environment along with suitable opportunities.

We can reject frustration, negative energy, boredom and other damaging psychological factors by working and developing our potential and skills. Leaders must help their people maintain their psychological balance, through continued care, encouragement and motivation.

The most important action we can take once we get rid of our negative energy is not to allow it to take hold of us again. There are several ways to do this, the most important of which is success, which cannot be attained without positive energy. When we succeed, we feel self-confident and eager to develop and excel.

---

1 Revisionism is a Marxist policy of revision or modification based on evolutionary socialist or pluralist principles, and is often used in a derogatory sense.

Part IV

EXCELLENCE IN DEVELOPMENT

CHAPTER TEN

Excellence in Dubai's Development Vision

Excellence in development is an integral concept, inherent to the vertical and lateral building process for us in Dubai. In order to achieve excellence in the Arab world, all the elements of development, including its vision, goals, leadership and implementation, should be excellent.

If excellence is an advanced stage of development, how can we establish excellence in those Arab societies that are less than exemplary? How can there be progress if their laws are not distinguished and neither are their goals, planning and behaviour? The list includes the public and private sectors, public and private schools, institutes and universities.

Some would argue that since not all human communities have achieved a state of excellence, why do we need excellence when we have to fund its high cost?

I will come to this question later, but what I can say right now is that, some development experiments in society are excellent and well advanced. We can study the essence of these experiments, the reasons behind their excellence and then design an advanced development concept of our own – one that we can successfully introduce in Arabia and other countries.

We could, of course, keep things the way they are, hoping luck would correct our path and put us on the right course. Like everyone else, I welcome luck; however I do not believe it presents itself every day and cannot wait for it to come knocking on my door!

The third option is to study our strengths and weaknesses and focus on promoting the first while eliminating the latter, until we reach a stage of balanced development, which we can then use as a fresh starting point in our drive towards quality and excellence.

Is this a dream or a vision?

I believe it is a mixture of both. Just like the development map of the rest of the world, the map of the Arab world is full of sharp differences, but ours are more specific to us. Some were the result of international political factors that resulted in a wide gap in development levels; others were differences in resources such as oil.

Although we can speak about the financial resources generated by energy exports, I personally prefer to speak about the ways these resources were spent.

Readily available finance does not necessarily mean development, because the real value of money lies in its efficient use and not its amount. A 12-million-dollar venture, for example, may generate a thousandfold return in just twenty years, while another similarly financed project may lose hundreds of millions of dollars in the same period. The difference between the two projects is the difference between a good idea and a bad idea, and between a mindset that seeks excellence and one that does not.

I do not mean to say that only people of certain nationalities or regions tend to generate excellent results, but rather, that we have never cultivated excellence in the Arab mind. If only we had invested as generously in minds as we have invested in projects that eventually failed... We have overloaded the back of the Arabian horse with all sorts of political, economic and social burdens, and then asked him to race against more agile and well-trained horses, expecting him to win.

Yet we Arabs can still win the race. We can still succeed and provide quality and excellence. We can still be pioneers. This is not simply a dream – we can achieve today what we have achieved in the past by reshaping the path we are using now. Development is an accumulative and integral process; a nutritional recipe for the nations of the world. If the recipe, ingredients and preparation are right, we will enjoy a terrific meal that carries the hallmark of quality.

The better the ingredients of the development process, the better the development we will enjoy, to a level that not only allows nations to compete and survive, but also allows them to take that giant step towards excellence.

I have said it before and I will say it again: people are the most important ingredient of the development process. If we fail to educate young people, develop their skills and generate the spirit of excellence and creativity in them, we will never, under any circumstances, have a successful development process.

The Arab failure in mastering the techniques of an efficient development process is a direct consequence of failing to care for people and coach them properly. There are several reasons for this, but we must admit that failure is in the first place, a failure in managing that process and failure of the leadership in directing the management. When it comes to national development programmes, one major failure could lead to dire consequences and an accumulation of such failures would be catastrophic. If sustaining development in such a vibrant world is a miracle, how do we go about achieving excellence in development?

God blessed us with a leadership of achievers, not egotists. When we compare our development experience in the United Arab Emirates with others, we find that there are some leaders who destroy their countries, while others promote the status and prosperity of their people. Our leaders walk down the streets without armoured cars and a large entourage of cars and motorcycles because they are not afraid of their people – they are one with them.

Those leaders keep their doors open for their citizens and are in close contact with them, so they feel and understand the pulse of the man in the street. With such a close and deep relationship between the leadership and the people, any decision taken by the former will be in the interest of the latter. This is the basis of a true vision – it is in the interest of the people.

On the other hand, if a leader sees only his entourage and palace, and has no contact with his people, their problems and aspirations, his vision, thoughts and decisions will move in one direction and those of his people will move in another.

Since the people are a leader's final reference, all his decisions and vision must serve their interests. When a leader gives precedence to this consideration over all others, he will succeed. Success means several things to us here in the UAE, one of which is achieving excellence. If a leader can achieve excellence by using the available resources, capacities and expertise, he should obviously do so, but, if they are not available, he must be prepared to cultivate them.

When a leader finds the right pillars to build excellence, he must immediately start building. If he cannot find them, he must be prepared to create them because a leader can only achieve excellence once he has invested effort, money, creativity and all other resources in developing his people.

A leader who wants to transform a vision into reality cannot be in two places at the same time and must either be in his palace or at the work site, heading the team. If such a leader takes the right decision he will find himself on the way to success and, if he keeps on course, he will undoubtedly reach excellence.

We in the UAE are on the road to excellence. The best advantage of success is that it is a sure way to achieving even more success.

Our vision was ambitious from the start, but our continued success encouraged us to aim even higher. When we compare our situation today with yesterday, we can feel and see the huge change that took place, and we can also see what is still left to achieve. We have accepted the challenge, survived the test and come out with our heads held high.

We have substantial resources and are highly determined and ready to use them. We want to be pioneers. We want Dubai to become a global centre for excellence and creativity. We want it to become the world's premier city for trade, finance, investment and tourism in the twenty-first century. We can provide the necessary infrastructure, services and environment and are confident that we can make this happen.

Here is the evidence.

Excellence in Management

Whoever studies the Dubai Government Excellence Programme is bound to be impressed. Management experts, who on several occasions have said that the programme is revolutionary in management reform, not only on the Arab level but also on the international level, were not exaggerating. Here is what they saw:

- Until recently, the private sector had been a better performer than the public sector, but the latter has recently started to tip the balance. For example, although the Dubai Quality Award[1] is dedicated to the private sector, many government departments have won the award.
- While the private sector has traditionally led in creativity, innovation and flexibility, the public sector is moving ahead in many aspects, including efficiency, initiative and excellence in service.
- Unlike the private sector, the public sector was known for its slow response, bureaucracy, low efficiency and poor achievement, but its efficiency is now better than that of many companies in the private sector.
- Although transparency was traditionally one of the features of the private sector, the public sector is continuously increasing its transparency. Businesses in the UAE and overseas can benefit from this.
- Corruption and bribery in the public sector is being dealt with ruthlessly. Mechanisms are in place to put an end to them throughout the sector and extra controls have been added to the sections dealing with projects, and financial and administrative affairs.
- There is a new commitment in the public sector with regard to the need for discipline, professionalism and in dealing with the public in a civilized manner.
- Some of the present government projects adopt hi-tech solutions and make them available, with other facilities, to the private sector, including Dubai Internet City and Dubai Media City.
- The public sector is implementing cost-effectiveness and resource management principles to achieve optimum performance, which will have a positive spin-off on the whole economy.

The excellence of the public sector is obvious through its ability to satisfy and serve the public. Our experience proves that this sector managed to achieve within six years what other countries would have needed many more years to accomplish.

How did the public sector manage to match the performance of the private sector in such a short time and why do we believe that it will move ahead and provide better services than the private sector? One of the reasons is that we have managed to extricate the public sector from routine and monotony, and put it on the path to modernity, development, increased productivity, greater performance, and respect for the public. This transformation was made possible by the people working in the sector. They developed themselves and their efficiency, were convinced of the need to stand up to their responsibility and achieved this transformation. They knew that it was in the interest of the country and the road to continued success.

The Dubai Government Excellence Programme was one of the tools used to achieve this. The programme was launched in 1997 with the aim of enabling the government sector to respond efficiently to the challenges of the new era we are living in. It also aims to upgrade the performance of government departments through continuous training and by fostering successful development experiences and procedures around the world.

This programme complements the Dubai Quality Award programme, which aims at promoting the concept of quality and adopting it in all fields.

The Government of Dubai itself does not select the winning department or define the performance excellence, but leaves this task to an independent committee of Arab experts who live abroad and are not connected with any of the Dubai government's departments in any way. These experts come to Dubai for a month or longer to assess the entries in all categories, according to established standards.

The committee then reports its findings and recommendations to the programme's management that adheres to the reports and announces the names of the winners in a special ceremony broadcast on TV and radio, and published in the press. This programme has become the driving force for the public sector and has promoted an unprecedented competitive spirit in government departments.

All civil servants, regardless of their position, compete for those rewards and no one wants himself or his department to come last.

Since some departments do not provide the names of all their good performers, we have established follow-up mechanisms that include 'undercover shopper' teams, whose members are specially trained to assess service levels at government departments. These members visit government departments as ordinary customers, and write down their remarks about the level of service and the promptness and precision of the civil servants in charge of dealing with the public.

This team also checks the commitment of the civil servants, their appearance, their ways of dealing with the public, eagerness to serve and work, productivity, computer proficiency and handling of complaints among others.

Recommendations might involve senior civil servants, but could also include lower-level employees, such as a blind telephone operator, an employee at the public relations section, a crane operator or any young national who may not be represented in the programme's categories. This mechanism has increased competitiveness. Now everyone seems eager to serve the public in the best way they can, in the hope that one of them is an undercover shopper, who can help him on his way to a promotion.

It is only normal in such a competitive environment that every department or section head says that his department or section is the best and deserves the award more than the others. That is why there is a tertiary assessment level that examines the public's opinion about the standards of services, since the public is the final judge. The survey's findings are published on an annual basis and contribute to improving performance.

The programme is performing successfully and I will continue monitoring its performance and upgrading it. I am also looking forward to promoting the interests of departments in the programme's seminars and training courses, and encouraging even better attendance by departmental heads and employees alike.

Excellence in integration

The UAE's economy is the most transparent and liberal in the Arab world, and the one most closely linked to free-market factors. The country's public sector is therefore at the service of the people and the private sector. It is not competing against the latter and never will. The performance of most government-owned companies and corporations is comparable to that of similar private businesses, but this does not justify the expansion of the public sector at the expense of the private sector – nor reducing the latter's share of the national economy.

Improving the performance and productivity of the public sector is not done with the intention of weakening or substituting the private sector's leading role in manufacturing, trade and services – it is simply not the role of the public sector in Dubai and never will be.

Generally, the public sector plays regulatory and supervisory roles. This role constitutes extending guidance, monitoring appropriate compliance to rules and regulations, and assuring commitment to quality control standards. On the other hand, the public sector must eliminate obstacles, facilitate services and reduce bureaucracy to a minimum. It is a simple and direct principle: enhanced performance leads to increased productivity, increased productivity speeds up the economic cycle, and speeding up the economic cycle will benefit the private sector and the people.

When the government establishes new economic entities such as Dubai Internet City, Dubai Industrial City,[2] Dubai Healthcare City[3] and Dubai International Financial Centre, it does not intend to operate these entities as government departments, but wants to provide a sophisticated environment where private businesses can operate, improve their productivity and profits, and provide job opportunities.

One of the main goals of the Dubai e-government initiative is to redefine the concept of government and allow it to become more efficient and active through the use of the Internet. Simplifying procedures is the basis for improving services, which is precisely one of the goals of electronic government. Among other major goals is upgrading the quality of services, reducing costs and mistakes, increasing the speed of response, providing services and information through the World Wide Web, elimination of routine and bureaucracy, and serving business communities whenever, wherever, and however they want.

Dubai's private sector is renowned worldwide for its dynamic power, resilience and ability to develop new markets, create opportunities, and expand all around the world. The new global economy provides Dubai with opportunities that never existed before. Energizing the traditional economy must therefore go hand in hand with the introduction of new economic sectors, such as electronic trade and online shopping.

This must further be accompanied by proper training for the new technologies involved and adopting modern working methods. Dubai must excel in its trade, services and economy in the digital age just as it did earlier.

The success of the government's initiatives aimed at energizing the public sector, and enabling it to deal with the new economy and digital technologies, is possible only through full coordination and cooperation between the government and the private sector. Since the government took the initiative of introducing new technologies and methods to the public sector on a large scale, the private sector seems keen on following suit in order to improve the quality of products and services in local and foreign markets.

The final goal of both the public and private sectors is to develop the local economy, to serve local and overseas markets and to provide consumers with the best services possible. The public sector, however, has the additional task of allocating investments and implementing projects that strengthen the economy and expand the market. When this happens, the private sector increases its share of the economy, its income and profits. This, in turn, generates more projects and job opportunities.

The success of the public sector is also a success for the private sector. Maintaining this success depends largely on the ability of the two sectors to develop a close partnership. This should allow for an exchange of experiences and expertise through permanent, open dialogue. An advanced public sector can provide quick, value-added services to the private sector. In turn, the private sector can contribute to the development of government departments and supply them with expertise such as training civil servants on the latest technologies available in their respective fields. Representatives of the private sector can also sit on government committees in order to improve their own efficiencies, keep pace with the latest developments and exchange expertise.

Both the public and private sectors share a common goal in the need to increase productivity and improve performance and efficiency. When both sectors agree on the need to improve services to consumers in local and overseas markets, their mutual coordination will improve economic performance. And the more this strategic partnership takes hold, the better the economy will perform.

We must also pay attention to one important point in all that we do. When we speak about the public and private sectors, we are not referring to two drivers pulling in opposite directions, but are rather speaking about two drivers pulling in the same direction, working in perfect harmony to speed up the production cycle and consequently, boost the economy.

This is the economic harmony we need to cross the economic hurdles and pitfalls that obstruct the road of international development from time to time.

Excellence in investment

I believe the country's investment goals will not merely be met when the country succeeds in attracting foreign investment, when a minister succeeds in convincing an investor to invest in the country, or when a corporation convinces a multinational to invest in new ventures in the country. We will achieve these goals only when investors succeed and make profits.

We are here to enable investors to succeed in their endeavours. If they fail we will fail with them, and if they succeed, we will flourish with them.

A manager of a company who recently relocated in Dubai asked me about our expectations from his company. I told him, "We expect you to succeed."

Development is a major objective by itself and national cooperation is useful, but what really interests an investor is the return on his investments. If an investor comes to Dubai, invests in a certain project and makes a million, he will respond by investing two million. If he makes a profit of two million, he will invest four million, and stories of success spread fast.

Dubai is not an oil-dependent emirate. Oil represents only a tiny percentage of our GDP. Our development projects are either self-financed, financed through Islamic loans, or through bonds floated in Dubai's or Europe's financial markets. There are tens of thousands of projects in Dubai and once you are an investor here, you are always an investor. You expand from your Dubai headquarters into other markets worldwide. Such investors know through experience that we will eliminate all obstacles obstructing their success, and their businesses will grow in an environment full of confidence, hope and great expectations of high returns.

Attracting foreign investment requires an accountable, transparent and ethical government sector. Unless governments eradicate corruption, they will never attract foreign investment. Most foreign companies cannot offer bribes because they would be violating the laws of their home countries and make their officials liable to serious penalties.

If a company cannot secure a deal through the proper channels, its officials should withdraw and if it knows that the country where it is intending to work is plagued by corruption, it would be better for it not to enter into dealings with that country from the outset. All the talk about offering incentives to investors and proclaiming laws that attract investments would be futile if we do not put an end to corruption. This is exactly what we have done in Dubai.

A distinguished investor does not only invest, establish companies and provide job opportunities; he also promotes expertise, competition, diversity and excellence. Such an investor brings us a modern business culture and new professional practices. He also expands the prospects of ushering in new markets, provides resident investors with new opportunities and contributes to finding solutions flexible enough to accommodate our own situations.

Foreign investors contribute to promoting our international reputation and pave the way for us to enter new markets overseas. That is why we must respect such investors and do whatever we can to help them succeed. This is how we have considered foreign investment in the past, how we consider it today, and how we will consider it in the future. We had an exclusive approach to foreign investments in the past and will have an even more exclusive approach in the future.

Since an important part of Dubai's philosophy is 'living the future today', we believe that Dubai offers one of the world's best investment opportunities, for the following reasons:

- No corporation income taxes.
- No income tax.
- No tax withholding.
- No tax on capital profits.
- No currency restrictions.
- No trade barriers.
- Low import duty (5 per cent) and many customs exemptions.
- Competitive salaries, home and office rents and operational costs.
- Additional preferential advantages for investors in Dubai's free zones such as the Jebel Ali Free Zone, Dubai Internet City, Dubai Media City, Dubai International Airport and scores of others. The advantages include allowing foreign investors 100 per cent ownership rights of their assets, repatriation of capital and profits, tax and customs duties exemptions and others. This has led to a huge surge in the number of companies established in such zones, currently exceeding 4,000 companies from more than 100 countries, with a total investment in excess of AED 44 billion (US$12 billion).
- Open markets and a free business environment.
- Investment returns in Dubai are among the best in the world. The flow of direct foreign investment has played a major role in the economy's impressive performance between 2001 and 2006. This included major economic sectors such as construction, real estate, manufacturing,

services and others. We expect this flow to continue unabated, with foreign investors and companies trying to benefit from the flow of large projects we are implementing now or planning for the future. This was accompanied by a consistent rise in the confidence of the international business community in both Dubai's and the region's economies and their future prospects.

- An advanced infrastructure matching those in the world's centres of excellence such as Europe, Japan and the United States of America. This includes ultra-fast communications, transport networks, airports, hotels and others.
- Benefiting from the commercial and marketing potential of one of the Middle East's best trade, manufacturing, finance and marketing hubs, with an annual overall trade of AED 550 billion (US$150 billion), serving markets of more than two billion consumers.
- Proven immunity from international economic crises. Dubai's economy kept growing despite the decline in the Japanese and European economies, as indicated by the following:
  a. On an average, GDP has grown by 12 per cent annually during the past 10 years, despite the consistent fall in oil receipts, rising from AED 44 billion (US$12 billion) in 1996 to AED 136 billion (US$37 billion) in 2005, almost doubling every three years.
  b. The Emirates Group[4] enjoyed record returns in the financial year ending 31 March 2005, reaching AED 19 billion (US $5 billion), a 36 per cent increase over the previous year's returns of AED 14 billion (US$3.8 billion).
  c. The number of passengers using Dubai International Airport grew by 14 per cent in 2005, compared with the previous year, reaching 24.6 million passengers.[5]
  d. Airfreight grew by 20 per cent in 2005, reaching 1.4 million tonnes, against 1.1 million tonnes in 2004.[6]
  e. Containers handled by DP World jumped sixfold in a decade, to reach more than 7.6 million containers in 2005.[7] The company is

now the Middle East's largest port operator, the world's seventh largest port operator and the world's fastest growing port operator. This promotes Dubai's status as the region's largest strategic hub for business and shipping, hosting some 100 shipping lines serving the world's largest markets.

f. Consistently healthy growth in the number of international exhibitions and conferences hosted by Dubai, made possible by the country's sophisticated infrastructure, security and safety, and its advanced and extensive MICE (meetings, incentives, conventions and exhibitions) facilities. The UAE has become the location of choice for exhibitors to display their latest products and business visitors to find all their needs under one roof. Some international exhibition experts believe, for example, that the Dubai Air Show is one of the world's three most important, growing by 12–20 per cent with each bi-annual show.

g. Real estate investment is one of the world's most rewarding. Land prices have jumped by forty times in some areas of Dubai during the last ten years. We expect this sector to play a crucial role in the growth of our GDP in the future, now that it has become the most dynamic in the Middle East and one of the most important in the world.

h. The value of the tourism, hospitality and catering sectors rose to AED 4.4 billion (US$1.2 billion) in 2004 compared to AED 3.68 billion (US$1billion) in 2003. More than five million guests stayed at Dubai's hotels in 2004, proof of the high level of safety, security, services and facilities that the emirate provides its residents and visitors alike.

i. The manufacturing sector grew by 15 per cent in 2005 to exceed AED 16.5 billion (US$4.5 billion), growing threefold in a decade.[8] We expect this sector to witness a quantum leap soon, through the establishment of Dubai Industrial City, which will cover an area of 560-million square feet, and provide opportunities to establish warehousing, distribution and after-sales service centres, serving the markets of the Central World Economic Zone which commands some two billion consumers living in the GCC, Central Asia, the Orient, Turkey, Cyprus and East and North Africa.

- An efficient, trustworthy and impartial government sector.
- Efficient response to the needs of investors, by providing what we call 'the single government services window'. This facility helps facilitate and expedite the procedures of setting up business in Dubai, including legal requirements, permits and other services. This service is so efficient and convenient, that more than half of the world's 1,000 largest companies have made Dubai their regional headquarters.
- While multinationals spend billions to recruit the skills needed to implement their projects, Dubai has one of the world's largest pools of international skills in one centre.
- An exclusive lifestyle and work environment in extensively equipped, ultra-modern residential and office developments.
- Exclusive exhibition facilities, including hi-tech, world-class complexes, hosting 100 major events each year.
- Exclusive services provided by the Dubai Development and Investment Authority to dedicated investors, entrepreneurs and businessmen wishing to move to Dubai, including:
  a. Implementing, developing and supporting dedicated, ambitious ventures that benefit from government subsidies in order to reduce the risks and challenges they might face;
  b. Attracting multinationals through appealing offers facilitating their move to Dubai;
  c. Supporting world-class local companies through attractive offers to develop their businesses, provide them with expertise, and enter into partnership agreements with them, in order to give them access to world-class clients.

Excellence in marketing

One of the reasons behind the continued success of the annual Dubai Shopping Festival[9] and the Dubai Summer Surprises events,[10] which attract millions of visitors, is that we do not only use these events to market only goods and services, but to market them within the framework of the city's excellence.

This involves turning these events into mega events celebrating Arab families, mothers, fathers and children alike, through scores of daily events aimed at a variety of visitors. They also celebrate technology, good conduct, honesty, good reputation, imagination, culture and entertainment.

Publicity is crucial to let people know what services we are providing and what events we have organized, to allow Dubai's residents and visitors to allocate their time in a way that allows them to benefit most from these two events. Visitors are, however, smart enough to distinguish between the exclusive and the ordinary, and know from the first contact that Dubai's reputation for excellence goes beyond its publicity.

Anyone visiting the city realizes from touchdown that Dubai is exclusive and different. Because Dubai's officials are deeply aware of the fact that first impressions count, they take great care in meeting visitors with a friendly and hospitable welcome at the airport, and provide them with all the assistance they need.

Dubai's reputation for excellence is a treasure we must cherish and protect. People trust the opinion and assessment of people they know more than what they see or hear from other sources. People will always trust those who maintain their good reputation, and the latter will consequently benefit through a higher market share, sales and profits. Those who do the opposite will find themselves out of business. Honest dealing creates the best publicity a salesperson or service provider can wish for.

Marketing is an integral process in which all must participate. It is an ongoing process and therefore needs a constant introduction of new talent, better qualified to perform their roles, innovate, diversify and introduce the latest techniques to attract consumer attention. It is a process that says the customer is always right and makes sure that all the products and services provided to him are of the top quality. Let us always remember that providing high quality is no more expensive than providing inferior quality.

Our marketing strategy targets four categories: visitors, residents, trade manufacturing and services, and export markets. We are organizing our development efforts with the help of dedicated personnel trained to understand the needs of citizens, residents, businessmen and visitors alike. We must not wait for customers to come to us, but should rather go to them in their own country. We must also focus on attracting new categories of visitors such as businessmen, executives and frequent travellers.

It is also important that we market the positive aspects of the emirate, using both its natural and sophisticated attractions, providing plenty of surprises while projecting a true and credible picture. Tourism marketing must go hand in hand with the availability of quality facilities. It is simply not acceptable that we organize tourism exhibitions around the world, allocate vast promotional budgets and encourage people to visit Dubai, only for them to face difficulties at the airport, or an inadequate number of taxis or hotel rooms.

Coordinating marketing exercises produces better results at a lower cost. We must avoid confused messages when we draft our marketing plan for international tourism-marketing events. Marketing plans should rely on field surveys in order to adequately understand the needs and priorities of potential tourists and facilitate their access to our market as well as the facilities and advantages we have on offer.

We have learned from our own experience that travel companies opt for attractive markets that provide amusement and entertainment more than markets that do not. Shopping and retail centres represent new investment opportunities and also attract tourists, and when such businesses are established in our market they play an important role in persuading others to follow. This has been crucial to our economic growth.

Dubai is the world's largest re-export market and we have a department dedicated to promoting our trade sector worldwide. The Dubai Tourism and Commercial Marketing department (DTCM) manages Dubai's marketing and promotional activities from offices in the Americas, Europe, Africa and Asia. We must, however, get more involved in marketing our

During the 'Spirit of the Union' lecture.

With a new batch of graduates at the American University in Dubai.

Meeting local and federal government department officials.

Listening to a brief on road developments in Dubai.

During a meeting of the Dubai Executive Council.

With my sons (from right) Saeed, Mansoor, Majid and Ahmed.

Unveiling Dubai 2010 Development Plan at the Dubai Strategic Forum.

Launching Dubai e Government.

Unveiling Dubai Media City.

Announcing the launch of Dubai Healthcare City project.

Announcing the launch of Dubai International Financial Centre.

Attending the Young Arab Leaders Forum.

During the Dubai Government Excellence Programme Awards ceremony.

At the 10th Annual Conference of The Emirates Center for Strategic Studies and Research.

Listening to a brief on Downtown Dubai projects.

Palm Jumeirah Island.

Burj Al Arab.

Emirates Towers.

Dubai Creek Golf and Yacht Club.

Inspecting Emirates Airline's A380.

Visiting Dubai International Airport.

At the Dubai International Airshow.

Examining the latest aviation technologies.

With graduates of the Mohammed bin Rashid Programme for Leadership Development.

Honouring winners of the Dubai Government Excellence Programme Awards.

Honouring winners of the Rashid Award for Academic Excellence.

Addressing a group of young UAE businesswomen.

Visiting the General Directorate of Residency and Foreigners Affairs in Dubai.

During a visit to Carrefour. UAE youth are encouraged to seek job opportunities in the private sector.

Visiting the Emirates Institution for Advanced Science and Technology (EIAST).

With winners of the Arab Journalism Awards.

An inspection visit to the Dubai Police Operations Room.

Visiting a private healthcare centre in Dubai.

The Dubai World Cup is the most prominent horse race in the world.

We are keen on attending major international horse races.

With my daughter Maitha and sons (from left) Ahmad, Hamdan, Rashid and Majid following great wins achieved in the Asian Games in Doha, Qatar.

With my daughters Maryam (left) and Shaikha.

During an endurance race with my sons (from left) Hamdan, Rashid and Maktoum.

Children of today are leaders of tomorrow, therefore, education is among our topmost priorities.

With HH Sheikh Khalifa bin Zayed during a falconry trip, joined by Mansur bin Zayed (leftmost) and my son Hamdan.

Falconry is a traditional sport that is very close to my heart.

Interacting with senior citizens during a visit to the Elderly Care Home in Ajman.

A visit to the Elderly Care Home in Ajman.

Inspecting the construction site of a new hospital in Fujairah.

Winning the gold medal at the World Endurance Championships in the UK.

exports and should have a presence in most countries. Direct contact is known to be the most effective way for building business partnerships and attracting investments, especially in countries such as Africa that depend on Dubai for a substantial part of their import requirements.

Serving the people is a serious responsibility and trade and service entities must abide by a code of conduct and strive to remain within certain limits. These goals should be achieved in an environment of positive and fair competition. Such an environment ought to provide shoppers with the opportunity to purchase whatever goods and services they like, without falling prey to fake or counterfeit goods, or any other unlawful practices.

Excellence in managing resources and cost efficiency

We have seen that quality service is more profitable than normal service, provided we master the art of managing resources and obtaining maximum efficiency from costs. For example, if Emirates Airline is providing a quality service and its competitor is providing a normal one, which airline is paying the higher price?

The competitor, of course, because it is not providing a quality service and is costing its government billions in losses. Emirates, on the other hand, is providing quality service and makes profits, not only in favourable, times but also when the whole aviation industry is in recession, such as in the aftermath of the tragic events of 9/11.

A second example: Dubai's hotels rank among the most luxurious in the world, so are their profits lower than those providing normal services? Definitely not, because the returns of the latter are lower than those of Dubai's hotels, not on the level of the Arab region alone but also on the international level.

A third example: which is costlier, a quality built factory or a non-quality one? If quality is not present in a factory, mistakes are bound to happen and mistakes are costly. If the mistakes resulted in the loss of human life, the cost would be exorbitant. Furthermore, the operational life of a non-quality factory is bound to be shorter than that of a quality one. Such a factory would never be able to provide quality and will find it difficult to market its products. Its returns will be low, and its working environment underdeveloped and harmful to people and the environment.

A fourth example: which government sector is costlier over the long term, the active or the lazy one? The active one of course. Here, however, we must bear in mind that the measure is no longer profit and loss because this applies only to the private sector. The public sector's efforts to upgrade its performance and services involves a strong commitment to cost efficiency and maximizing the benefits resulting from the labour of human resources and other available resources such as work places and computer systems.

If we have an open hall, we must endeavour to optimize its use by allocating the best place to the personnel that are going to work in it, and by providing them with working conditions that allow them to be more productive and innovative. Naturally, we should also optimize the use of computer systems through all kinds of networks linking them to other departments and with to the Internet.

We are not constantly encouraging creative initiatives and developing new ideas, just for the sake of gathering theoretical data. We are providing them to work teams to study and implement practical proposals that reduce costs and increase revenue. Governments that want to succeed have no choice other than to make all their departments act as teams to achieve common goals, without complication or duplicity.

They can do this by joining forces with their personnel and encouraging them to contribute to their plans, initiatives and programmes. For example, I know of one suggestion that saved a department AED 10 million, while another that suggested imposing a fractional charge on installing computers generated a steady income from banks to another department. Reducing operational cost in the public sector relieves the budget, although other material and moral targets are equally important.

The efficiency of the government sector does not only affect the performance of the public sector – it affects that of the whole country, including the private sector. When the public sector's achievements pick up speed, the increased pace extends to the activities in all other sectors: incorporating new companies, implementing projects, and imports and exports, to name a few. Efficient resource management is essential to secure our future and economic sustainability; therefore, we must continually emphasize the importance of this principle.

Some managers were relieved following the implementation of the Dubai e-government programme, thinking it was time to relax and take a break – but the opposite was true. What is the use of giving somebody a TV set if he cannot operate it? Acquiring technology does not mean that we have reached the end of the road; in order to optimize our benefit, mastering the use of technology is even more important than acquiring it.

This is not restricted to service providers only – it also covers their users. We have, therefore, constituted a work team in charge of training the users of the e-government's portal. We will endeavour to expand the use of the portal and facilitate its access for more time and cost efficiency.

Companies and individuals can use the time they save to increase productivity, enjoy more free time with the members of their families, or for cultural activities or entertainment. This, in turn, contributes to enriching social relations and excellence.

Excellence in coexistence

Often when I am alone in my car in the streets of Dubai, I have a feeling I cannot clearly explain, something akin to the transparency of dawn or the shadows of night. I like to think of it as the 'spirit of Dubai' – a blend of the spirit of the city and the spirit of its inhabitants.

If a man can smile to himself, it will be easy for him to smile at others. This is how the residents of Dubai are. The first step towards smiling is in freeing people of negative energy, despair and frustration. This happens when a man makes an accomplishment, which then brings him joy and a sense of achievement. His morale will be boosted and he will interact positively with others.

Whoever lives in Dubai remains in Dubai. Even when people leave Dubai for another city, many of them come back. I have heard scores of stories about people who went to Canada, Europe or the United States, only to come back to Dubai after a couple of years, sometimes even sending their children ahead of them.

Some of our residents had humble beginnings before gaining an international reputation and status in business, and acquiring large companies. Others acquired their business skills in Dubai before they were recruited to highly paid jobs overseas, yet they came back to Dubai after gaining further skills and achieving good returns on their savings and investments abroad.

A friendly, tolerant atmosphere and established traditions, which everybody respects, prevail in Dubai. There is self-respect, mutual respect, sobriety, excellence and civilization.

You can walk safely through the city's streets and alleys anytime you wish. If you ever look behind you, it is not to see whether a thief or pickpocket is tailing you, as would be the case in many cities around the world; it would rather be to enjoy the distant lights of the city twinkling on the horizon, or looking for a face you may recognize. Some old-timers return to Dubai just for this reason: it is a safe city.

Dubai is distinguished by its clean streets, beautiful buildings and delightful public parks. We do not tell people what they should wear because there is a natural elegance and care about appearance and behaviour in those who appreciate excellence.

Thousands of people who have visited Dubai have returned as residents. Each one of them has a story to tell. One of them was a German dentist who graduated at Harvard and lectured at the University of Berlin. Following a visit to Dubai as a tourist, he liked the city's lifestyle and decided to come back as a resident and open a practice here. What is surprising about this is that he first visited Dubai in August (the hottest month of the year). Imagine visiting Dubai in August and deciding to live here over Germany and the University of Berlin!

Dubai enjoys an enviable lifestyle that only exists in certain coastal cities. There is constant change in Dubai because excellence does not know idleness. Dubai abounds with initiative, with the will to innovate and constant action day and night. Although everybody feels satisfied, there are admittedly the inescapable work pressures because everybody has to wake up early and start his daily race. Nevertheless, the day's labours are handsomely rewarded at night when there is ample entertainment to enjoy.

We have talked extensively about productivity, performance, efficiency and development, but we are not asking anyone to work at the expense of their family. We want them to do what they are paid to do. We want to be fair and deal in a civilized manner with people.

We want people to achieve balance in their lives, giving their jobs their due attention and time, and giving the same to their families and themselves, because the best time someone can have is time with their family. We want them and their families to enjoy life and entertain themselves, otherwise they will not be ready to join the race the following morning.

Children have an important place in Dubai because they have an important place in the hearts of Arabs, and the excellent services we are providing children with is no mean feat. It is of the same calibre that we are providing to adults, because excellence crosses all boundaries of age and race. Excellence should be made available to all, at all times and under all circumstances. Excellence is not restricted to trade and industry and should also be available in services.

There are jobs for women everywhere in Dubai. Women are held in great esteem, not only because they constitute half the society, but also because they are the mothers of society. Women are also held in such high esteem because they are taking part in our great race and winning on merit. Women are now leading work teams, managing the destinies of their companies and the lives of their children. They are achieving success, bringing up the future's younger generation, generating wealth and jobs, and even racing horses against men and beating them to the finishing line!

As mentioned briefly in chapter one, Cordoba, a city in Andalusia, Southern Spain, was under Moorish rule from 711–1236 AD. During this time of Islamic rule, Cordoba was the largest city and enjoyed the most sophisticated culture in Europe. It reached its peak in the tenth century when it boasted more than 1,000 mosques and 600 public baths. The most important monument in the city is the former Grand Mosque, one of the largest mosques in the world.

In Cordoba women were held in great esteem, just like in Dubai. A woman called Rusais used to ride on horseback, wearing a head cap and a sword, with the Caliph of Cordoba, Abdul Rahman Al Naser,[11] through the city's streets and beyond, to the city of Al Zahra.[12] Another woman called Lubnah was the secretary of the Caliph Al Hakam bin Abdul Rahman,[13] while yet another, Muznah, was the secretary of the Caliph Al Naser Lideen Ellah.[14] Historians have said Andalusian women exerted a great deal of influence and enjoyed much freedom in such an open society.[15]

Dubai is a city of options. Its residents can choose their own lifestyles and entertainment. Work in some of the world's renowned business cities is just work, but work in a city that adds tourism to the formula is a real pleasure. That is why Dubai has attracted a large number of talented people, the likes of which you will not find in any other single city.

There are also, of course, Arab expatriates living overseas. For more than fifty years we have been complaining about the drain of Arab minds and money to the West, but what have we done to stop this worrying trend? We have complained even more about the West, accusing it of stealing the resources and minds of our nations.

The West is not to blame. When an expatriate Arab returns home with his family for a holiday, for example, he can hardly go through the airport without regretting his decision to come home in the first place. Queues are endless, you have to wait between one and two hours in sweltering heat, eyes are scrutinizing him as if he is a criminal, while people are asking unnecessary questions. The expatriate searches left and right in vain, seeking to hide his sense of shame from the eyes of his wife and children.

If the gateway to home is like this, what will home look like? No one cares, smiles, helps, nor says, "*Marhaba*!" (welcome).

Talented Arab expatriates are very welcome in Dubai. We have welcomed many returning Arab expatriates this way and we will welcome many more in the future. To raise their children, some expatriates wanted an Arab environment with standards of education, health and services matching those in Europe and America. We have all this and more.

Others came back to obtain a high return on their investments, realizing Dubai offers excellent returns. Moreover, Dubai does not nationalize, confiscate nor trespass on other people's property, so we welcome Arab expatriate money.

Other expatriates from India, Pakistan, the US, Syria, Egypt, Britain, France, Australia, South Africa and more than 150 other countries find similar advantages and more in Dubai, and add that they have managed to blend fairly quickly into Dubai's society. I guess this is only normal because Dubai is a city where you do not feel estranged or marginalized and where nobody lives on the fringes feeling dismal, because this is a feeling alien to Dubai.

Dubai is a blend of Arab civilization and global aspirations for excellence, just like Cordoba used to be in the past. The number of universities in the capital of the second Umayyad Empire was just a notch less than the total number of universities in the rest of Europe at the time. Moreover, Cordoba's universities were so distinguished that many Europeans preferred them to their own universities and studied there to qualify for senior posts in their own countries. Some of them even became popes.

Scores of merchants from Europe, Asia and Africa were trading actively in the markets of that phenomenal city of more than one million inhabitants, including Muslims, Christians and Jews. The only golden age Jews ever knew in their ancient history was that with the Arabs of Andalusia. There were scores of Jewish philosophers, scientists, doctors and master craftsmen.

Here we discover yet one more of the distinguished aspects of excellence: when we respect the religion and faith of other people, they respect ours.

Respect is, however, not a gift and must be earned, so how can we convince other people that Islam is tolerant while some of us are not? How can we convince them about the fairness of Islam when some of us are oppressing others? How can we convince them that it is a just religion while some of us are unjust?

God says in his Holy Book, "Let there be no compulsion in religion." So what right do we have to force others to embrace our religion? We have to assume the responsibility of presenting people of other faiths with a beautiful picture of Islam. This can only be done by dealing with them positively, living with them in peace and harmony, and jointly achieving a successful economic and humanitarian development.

Excellence does not recognize religious or ethnic differences because its overwhelming humanitarian nature overcomes everything that might create differences between people. Every one of us wants to live in peace, work, produce and make profits in an environment that provides everybody with equal opportunities, rights and obligations. That is why maintaining peace and security is a responsibility we all share. It is the most important factor in maintaining production and protecting interests, together with all the other aspects of coexistence: coexistence of religions, different opinions, values and concepts.

Neither Al Hambra Palace in Grenada,[16] the Cordoba Great Mosque,[17] Madinat Al Zahra[18] nor the Seville Palace,[19] is the most important legacy of the Arab civilization in Andalusia. The real legacy of that civilization was that it provided mankind with the most unique example the world has known so far of the possibility of successful coexistence of civilizations and religions in an environment that allows everybody to cooperate in creating excellence.

But look at what took the place of Cordoba's scientific and academic institutions – the Inquisition. Cordoba's great cultural and literary period was followed by the mass burning of all sorts of books and the imprisonment of whoever was found reading one of them. Racism followed Cordoba's exemplary coexistence.

Most of the New World's civilizations have fallen victim to this kind of racism. The Spaniards never perceived the diversity of human civilization as one of the most beautiful aspects of humankind at the time and instead saw in it a ruthless and pitiless enemy.

The great diversity that exists nowadays in Dubai and the one that existed long ago in Cordoba are part of their strong appeal. This combination can take a different form in another place. Nearly 1,000 years after the fall of the caliphate rule in Andalusia's capital, we are providing another example of successful coexistence between different civilizations, religions and opinions, in a city where everybody is striving for excellence in all fields.

Whoever talks today about a war between civilizations, and about an enmity between Islam and the West, claiming that the West cannot coexist with Islam and that Muslims glorify death and not life, have evidently not visited Dubai nor heard about the history of Cordoba, or even that of all the great Arabian cities. All those cities were living examples of successful coexistence between all religions. We are today doing the same and providing proof once again that coexistence is what Islam calls for.

The history of our civilization stands witness to this.

---

1 The Dubai Quality Award is a process for recognizing role model organizations that provide other organizations with a roadmap to achieve excellence through the adoption of good practices and sound approaches, deployed systematically, and continuously measured and reviewed.

2 Dubai Industrial City is the industrial complex in Dubai dedicated to fostering the growth of manufacturing companies in the emirate, covering an area of 560 million square feet. When completed, the development will include a food and beverage zone; a transport equipment and parts zone; a machinery and equipment zone; a mineral products zone; a base metal zone; a chemicals zone; warehouses; and an extensive conservation area. It is located near Al Maktoum International Airport in Jebel Ali and is expected to accommodate around 500,000 people once fully operational.

3 Dubai Healthcare City is dedicated to healthcare excellence. It offers expertise across a wide range of specialities, and is home to major national and international healthcare brands. The city now hosts over 100 medical facilities and 3,000 healthcare professionals.

4 Emirates Airline and its associated companies.

5 The annual passenger traffic in Dubai International Airport reached 50.98 million in 2011, indicating an 8 per cent rise compared to 47.2 million recorded in 2010.

Passenger numbers are projected to reach 56.5 million by the end of 2012 and 98 million by 2020.

6 Dubai International Airport handled a total of 1,481,736 tonnes of freight between January and August 2012, indicating a 3 per cent increase compared to 1,438,044 tonnes recorded in 2011. On 27 June 2012, Dubai Airports launched cargo operations at Dubai World Central (DWC). DWC handled 106,333 tonnes of freight in the first half of 2012 compared to 32,634 tonnes in the first six months of 2011, marking a 226 per cent increase in cargo volumes.

7 In 2011, DP World, UAE Region, achieved the throughput of 13,000,000 TEU in a single year.

8 According to the *Dubai StatisticalYearbook (2010)*, the manufacturing sector contributed 13.2 per cent (AED 38,719 billion) to Dubai's GDP.

9 Dubai Shopping Festival (DSF) started on 15 February 1996 as a retail event intended to revitalize retail trade in Dubai. It has since been promoted as a tourist attraction. The month-long event is the region's largest shopping and entertainment extravaganza. In 2009 alone, visitors reached the 3.35 million mark and spent AED 9.8 billion.

10 Dubai Summer Surprises is the summer counterpart of DSF, held over ten weeks, and focusing on fun and education.

11 Abdul Rahman Al Naser (889–961) was the Emir and Caliph of Cordoba (912–961) of the Ummayad dynasty in Al Andalus. He ascended the throne in his early twenties and reigned for half a century as the most powerful prince of Iberia.

12 Al Zahra refers to the ruins of a vast, fortified Arab Muslim medieval palace-city built by Abdul Rahman Al Naser. Located on the western outskirts of Cordoba, Spain, it was the de facto capital of Al Andalus or Muslim Spain.

13 Al Hakam bin Abdul Rahman (915–976) was the second Caliph of Cordoba in Al Andalus and the son of Abdul Rahman Al Naser. He ruled from 961 to 976.

14 Al Naser Lideen Ellah (1158–1225) was the thirty-fourth Abbasid Caliph in Baghdad from 1180 until his death.

15 Ehsan Abbas (1969), *The History of Andalusian Literature – The Cordoba Dominance Era*, Beirut: Al Thaqafah, p. 25.

16 Al Hambra Palace, literally 'the red one', is a palace and fortress complex located in Granada, Andalusia, Spain. It was constructed during the mid-tenth century by the Berber ruler, Badis ben Habus of the Kingdom of Granada in Al Andalus.

17 The Cordoba Great Mosque, currently the Cathedral of Our Lady of the Assumption, is today a World Heritage Site. It is located in the Andalusian city of Cordoba, Spain. The mosque is regarded as the one of the most accomplished monuments of Islamic architecture.

18 Madinat Al Zahra is a town situated 13 kilometres northwest of Cordoba. It was also renowned for its highly advanced civilization and architecture.

19 The Seville Palace is a royal palace in Seville, Spain, originally a Moorish fort. It is the oldest royal palace still in use in Europe. In 1987, it was registered by UNESCO as a World Heritage Site.

CHAPTER ELEVEN

Made in Dubai

I would like to begin this chapter with some examples that illustrate a point that needs to be made, and then follow on from there...

- If we told someone fifteen years ago that we were considering developing tourism in Dubai, they would probably have fallen over laughing. Dubai now welcomes some six million tourists a year.[1] If we told that same person a few years later that we were planning to raise that figure to fifteen million tourists a year by 2010, he would probably have taken us more seriously. People realize now that when Dubai promises, Dubai delivers.
- A few years ago, there were two structures in the world that could be seen from space. The first of these was the Great Wall of China, and the second the Hoover Dam, commissioned in the United States by 1936. If we told people in 1977 that we intended to join China and the US and build a structure that could be seen from space, the response might have been, "Dream on!" But, by 1979, Dubai had commissioned the sixty-seven-berth Jebel Ali Port, the world's largest man-made port, which can be seen from space. This unique 'club' of structures visible from space has now been joined by The Palm Islands, the world's largest residential and tourism, man-made islands.
- All around the world, countries lose parts of their sandy beaches to provide space for ports and residential projects. We Arabs love our children and enjoy seeing them play on clean, soft sand. Once completed, The Palm and The World islands will have added hundreds of kilometres of beaches to Dubai's coast.
- Racehorses usually train and race in Europe, in an age-old tradition that no one dares to try to change. When we announced our intention to train our horses in an Arab country during the winter months, the racing fraternity protested. They said the proposal was outrageous, we would fail and our horses would never win. It seems some people did

not know us very well. The world's best horses are now being trained in Dubai. We fly them to Europe to take part in races and then fly them back home to their training base. Godolphin[2] has become world renowned in managing global horse racing operations and we are still winning races just like we used to.

- Some people not only predicted our Dubai Internet, Technology and Media project would fail but thought we were naive to even consider launching it, saying, "You have no Internet or technology to speak about, and cannot be considered a media hub, so how can you build a whole 'city' dedicated to Internet, technology and the media? You will be taking a massive risk if you do."

  I knew it was a risk and in my inaugural speech in 2000, I said, "The greatest risk for a man is not to take risks." Some people, on the other hand, did not realize the possibility of integrating the Internet and the media when we conceived the project and consequently, could not foresee the integration between the Internet and freedom of speech. Who was right and who was wrong? When I proposed the project, I invited a number of the world's most prominent technology companies to join. All those companies are now firmly established in Dubai Internet City, in addition to scores of others. If we had not taken the risk, the number of technology and media companies in Dubai would never have reached the 700 mark of today, we would never have turned the United Arab Emirates into one of the Middle East's most important Internet, technology and media hubs, and the media would not have enjoyed its present freedom.
- Money is the nerve centre of any economy, both new and traditional. The new economy, however, is distinguished by its quick tempo and requires a similarly quick response to financial transactions and the movement of international capital. That is why Dubai International Financial Centre was conceived in 2002. It is also there to complement Dubai Internet City, Dubai e-government, Dubai e-commerce and other hi-tech ventures.

There is a large gap in servicing the movement of international capital and financial markets in the economic centre running through the Middle East, Central Asia and the Indian Subcontinent. Dubai International Financial Centre will bridge that gap, creating a link for financial services between our region and international markets. It will provide a round-the-clock international trading system, which will include dealing in financial assets, stocks, insurance and reinsurance and large banking transactions.

- More than a trillion US dollars worth of Arab assets are invested in the US and Europe. We believe that Dubai International Financial Centre will provide the appropriate channels to repatriate some of those assets and contribute to developing Islamic banking services.

We want to support the centre by developing the Dubai Stock Exchange, in order to make it the region's prime market for financial papers, bonds and other financial tools, as well as one of the most important centres for raising capital to provide finance to all sorts of parties, including established companies and start-ups.

We want DIFC to excel and will therefore provide the stock exchange and the financial, investment and insurance companies operating there with an ideal work environment, including the necessary legal, regulatory and supervisory framework, matching the world's best. This step will put Dubai on a par with the world's most prestigious financial centres, including London and New York.

For this to happen, the legal framework must match that in force in other sophisticated international centres. Accordingly, I have written to the Regulatory Council of the Dubai Financial Services Authority, assuring them of "our strong commitment to providing the highest standards of transparency and good governance, in all aspects of the work of the Dubai Financial Services Authority. These standards are fundamental pillars of DIFC's success and efficiency. Consequently, we are instructing you to uphold such standards in all fields related to the Dubai Financial Services Authority".

- At a time when airlines were reducing the size of their fleets in order to reduce operational costs and manage the crisis that hit the industry following the 9/11 events, raising their losses to AED 113 billion (US$31 billion), we concluded a US$15-billion deal to purchase an additional fifty-eight aircraft. During the financial year ending March 2005, Emirates Airline had added nine new aircraft to its fleet, raising its total to fifty-seven, with an average age of 4.5 years. The airline is now planning to raise the total number of its jet-aircraft fleet to 150 (including twelve cargo planes) by 2012, to meet an expected rise in the number of passengers travelling the airline's routes to 33 million.
- When the public sector shakes off sluggishness, routine and monotony, it becomes a large group of active and creative cells boasting departments with innovative expertise and solutions that can be mutually beneficial in developing work methods and promoting better performance. The government sector directly impacts the progress of nations, because it leads and guides. If that sector is efficient and creative, there is no limit to its positive impact at all levels. We therefore expect that sector to play a vital role in realizing the vision of making Dubai a pioneering economic centre matching the best in the world. We also expect that sector to contribute more to the general budget. In 2004, for example, the contribution of the government services sector to the budget rose 4 per cent to AED 7.5 billion (US$2 billion). This would not have been possible without the efforts exerted by this sector to upgrade its performance and the standard of its service.

Now I have some questions:

- Which city in the Middle East has eight championship golf courses, with this number constantly growing?
- Which is the world's largest re-export market for right-hand drive cars?
- Which is the world's largest re-export market?
- Where is the highest office tower in the Middle East and Europe?
- Where is the Middle East's largest financial centre?

- Where is the Middle East's largest, and the world's fifth-largest, airport duty-free?
- Where is the Middle East's most active airport?
- Where is the world's largest independent aluminium smelter?
- Where is the Middle East's largest concentration of IT companies?
- Where is the Middle East's largest free zone?
- Where is the Middle East's largest media city?
- Where was the highest annual economic growth rate in the world recorded during the past ten years?
- Where is the Middle East's largest dry dock?
- Where is the world's tallest and most luxurious hotel?
- Where are the world's largest man-made islands?
- Where is the world's largest man-made port?
- Where are two of the world's four superstructures that can seen from space?
- Where do you expect the world's tallest tower has been built?[3]
- Where do you expect the world's largest shopping mall has been built?

I will stop here and review some common points between these projects:

- **They all involve risks:** A major risk looms behind every big opportunity, although there is a major difference between calculated risks and economic suicide. All our major projects are subject to intensive feasibility studies by dedicated international consultants. Excellence in implementing a project means you must be right from the outset, in every respect. This is what we are always trying to achieve while acknowledging the risks.
- **They pose challenges:** Challenges inspire determination, reinvigorate willpower and keep the mind alert. Most of our achievements are just samples of what will follow in the future. They are a test of our ability to face new challenges, because our vision for the future is far-reaching. We must always be alert and ready to avail ourselves of any emerging opportunities or if necessary, make them ourselves. Our work team

must acquire all possible expertise to solve the problems we expect to meet on our way to excellence. If we do not find the right challenges, we should make them, because they are the best training our work teams can have.

- **They reflect excellence:** Because Dubai is a city of excellence, its projects must reflect excellence in concept, taste and practice, and they should also reflect elegance. An engineer once said that when he walks through the streets of some of the Middle East's cities, he tends to think the architects of those cities did not enjoy their profession, because he does not see any beauty or creativity in their designs. But anyone visiting Abu Dhabi or Dubai will realize architectural competition has produced unique levels of excellence and creativity. When you have an excellent start, more excellence is bound to follow; it will become more comprehensive and will never stop developing.
- **They reflect originality in design:** We draw some of our architectural designs from our environment and heritage. The aptly named Burj Al Arab (Tower of the Arabs) was designed in the form of the sail of a traditional Arab dhow. The Palm Islands were designed in the shape of date palms, complete with fronds. The Jumeirah Beach Hotel was designed in the form of the crest of a wave. We always endeavour to include symbols of our heritage in the design of our buildings, while considering aesthetics, functionality and practicality, and maintaining top professional standards.
- **They change prevailing concepts:** Our architecture looks at things from different points of view. What is right or good from one point of view might not be so from another. What is prevailing and established might not be the best you can get, and what might be whimsical for me could be realistic for others. What is important though is that you should look around and question the reason for the existence of what you're able to see. And it is even more important to think about the things you cannot see – and consider the reasons for their absence.

The Burj Al Arab is a good example. Some of those who heard about the plans for the hotel said they were unsuitable because nobody had thought about it beforehand. We, on the other hand, considered it realistic and built it because it would promote Dubai's excellence and would consequently be beneficial to its people.

Some people have proposed projects to us that they considered excellent but which we rejected. We want the right mettle, which explains why we sometimes see things from a different perspective – which brings me to my second example, The Palm Islands. These three large, man-made islands will face Jumeirah Beach, Jebel Ali and Deira. Whoever owns a home overlooking the sea is fortunate, but owning a home at sea, overlooking the beach, is really out of the ordinary. Whoever lives on one of these islands will be living on one of the wonders of the New World.

- They make markets: If you are in Africa and wanted Japanese goods, do you order them from Tokyo or Dubai? From Dubai of course! Would you guess that we are exporting French perfumes to Tunisia? Would you believe that senior French officials passing through Dubai Duty Free buy French perfumes which, they concede, are much cheaper than in their country of origin?
- These examples illustrate Dubai's ability to find markets for goods it does not even produce. I would also like to include two more examples. As previously mentioned, although the cars in Dubai are left-hand drive, we are the world's largest market for second-hand, right-hand drive cars, re-exported to world markets. The second example is that despite living in a desert where rain seldom falls and where most of the land is unsuitable for farming without special treatment, we have the world's largest vegetable market.
- They either self finance themselves or float IPOs and bonds on the Dubai or international stock exchanges.
- They require new technologies and high-calibre expertise to implement.
- They are implemented in record time.

- They reflect a high level of effort and coordination between work teams.
- They reflect foresight, making use of opportunities and even making opportunities when necessary.
- They are capable of overcoming crises: Setting priorities and adopting growth and expansion strategies does not mean putting yourself in a straightjacket. Such priorities must be flexible and capable of accommodating emergency changes. For example, when the Second Gulf War disrupted air traffic worldwide, Emirates Airline quickly rode the storm and its jets were grounded for only five hours in Europe.
- They are bridges to other projects: We have many new projects which will be implemented in due course, within the framework of our strategy to build the future of our country. We consider these new projects the gateway to international status in management.
- They put an end to prevailing Western concepts, such as the belief that there is an advanced North, a backward South, an outstanding West and a not-so-distinguished East.
- They prove that Dubai and the Arab people are capable of implementing projects of international standards that match or even overtake similar ones in the West or East.
- They free human imagination because they involve a great deal of imagination in the way of thinking, concept and achievement.
- They are of the highest international standards: The work environment should not mean traditional offices, computers and continuously ringing telephones. When we first thought about establishing Dubai International Financial Centre, we pondered for quite a long time on the use of the word 'international'. We found that the project had a great deal of 'globalization' in all its aspects. A large number of the 55,000 people who will work and live in the centre would be expatriates. We want each and every one of them to feel at home from the moment they move in. We have added touches of excellence to the project so that these people will feel privileged to work in a unique place, the likes of which simply do not exist anywhere else around the world.

The main goal is to provide a working and living environment of international standard – two separate worlds that coexist in the same place; a place of excellence and creativity. Outside the offices of the international, regional and local exchanges and financial and investment companies, you will find a blend of high-rise towers and traditional quarters with an international touch: an opera house, theatres, libraries, parks and fountains. Cars, noise and smoke will be conspicuous in their absence. We believe that the 'modernization tax' imposed in most of the world's other international financial centres is not welcome in Dubai and it is our intention to exempt all those who embrace Dubai International Financial Centre as their new world from having to pay it.

The Dubai way

If we wanted to summarize the previous paragraphs, we could say that these projects represent the 'Dubai way of doing things', consisting of:

- Crystallizing the vision;
- Setting the goals;
- Drawing the plan;
- Setting a reasonable time for implementation;
- Mobilizing resources;
- Giving the signal for implementation of the project.

The Dubai way of doing things means that work is undertaken according to Dubai's concept of excellent achievement, and to specific standards, requirements and specifications, some of which are as follows:

- Superiority: Dubai teaches us that true excellence does not come from being superior to others, but means surpassing oneself time and again. This is achieved by going the extra mile when one believes they have reached the end of the road.

  It is the extra effort one puts into work when they believe it is time for a break; the extra time one spends thinking about work outside of working hours; and the extra contribution one makes when they think they have already given everything. It is the finishing touch an artist gives to a painting, when he steps back to look at it and then adds the final touch that catches the attention of critics. It is also the continuous belief that there is something extra one can add but are not sure exactly what it is and keep searching for it until its found. Surpassing oneself also means forgetting all about the word 'despair', maintaining hope, thinking positively and having the will to succeed.

- Overcoming the impossible: There is no single definition for the word 'impossible'. One might find that what they considered impossible ten years ago is possible today, and what is impossible for one person is not so for another.

  If I cannot overcome something, the reason could be that I have never found an appropriate way to do so. The way to conquer the impossible is to refuse to concede to despair and say, "Somewhere, somehow, there is a way… so let us find out what it is."
- The melting pot of success: Any success or failure is always collective. Every member of each work team must be aware that the success of his team depends on his own success, and that the success of his team is crucial for the success of other teams. Management must know that failure to mobilize the potential of all the teams to achieve set targets will lead to the failure of those teams. The leader must realize that if he does not lead the ranks and guide everybody in the construction process, there will be no success.

  When expertise, skills, work pace and integration are achieved, you will not only have a group of highly efficient work teams or an efficient management, but a consolidated and efficient work team. We have such a team in Dubai, the largest of its kind in the Middle East. Behind this team is, however, an even larger one made up of Dubai's residents. That is why I say without any hesitation that it is the largest team of its kind anywhere in the world.

What project would be impossible for such a team? Would the team not say, "We will make it happen and turn it into a success story!"?

- Civilized models of management: Management reform in Dubai was an experience, but is now a school. There are several ways to execute a task, but we opted for a distinguished, high-performance, highly modern management school. We believe that our people deserve to be treated in the best manner, befitting them and their age-old civilization. We shall never cease calling upon Arab countries and managers to benefit from mature and comprehensive development and management experiences instead of adapting other schools of thought from other countries, only to realize after some time that they were not the right models for developing our societies.

  This happened in the past and we are still reeling from its impact, but it must not happen in the future. We want to share Dubai's experience in developing better government departments and introducing managerial reforms. We would like our experience to contribute to upgrading the Arab administrative system and encourage excellent government performance. We want to serve all Arabs in any way we can.
- Creating circumstances for success: I have previously stated that we should not be in a rush because development is a creative process. We could wait for favourable winds before weighing anchor, but this is not the only option. Some projects are born naturally following careful consideration, planning, and studying all the details and options. Other projects require quick action. There may not even be time for a feasibility study because the various stages have to be completed in record time.

  This applies even more to the new economy than the traditional one. Information technology or e-commerce projects have a different motto: 'First come, first served' or even 'First come, first to stay'. We have seen several outstanding examples in recent years, including Amazon, eBay, Google, Microsoft and others. In such cases, we solve the problems as they appear. This, however, requires an experienced team of achievers with a proven track record of dependability in challenging situations.

- Positive attitude: Dubai is in an era of positive change that contributes to promoting positive attitudes throughout our region and beyond. We are not Hong Kong, Singapore, the Silicon Valley or any similar place. We have different visions and priorities. We contribute to the development of the UAE. We are what we are, with all our positive attitudes and contributions that we are seeking to build on, and our negative attitudes that we are trying to eradicate with more work, optimism, self-confidence and positive energy. Religion for us is also a way of life. We are committed to the edicts of our religion and see no conflict between them and modernization and true civilization. We are not going to do anything at the expense of our religion, because we will then be left without a religion – and without our religion, we would be without a world.
- Innovation: It could be argued that there are no sacred human laws and regulations. They were established in order to regulate certain things on certain occasions. Since development means continuity, these laws and regulations could become obsolete sometime in the future, and may obstruct development instead of securing a streamlined form of progress. Free zones provide successful tools for overcoming legal and regulatory obstacles, but this process cannot happen haphazardly.

No matter how good expertise is, there will always be something better. When I decided to invite foreign companies to invest in Dubai, I could not dictate what they would have to do. They know better than me how to succeed.

The best solutions are sometimes the easiest. Since we want to make things easier for multinationals and ourselves, and we want them to succeed as quickly as possible, we asked them for a 'wish list' of what they expect and we endeavour to meet those wishes and remove all obstacles, within the limits of our laws, regulations and procedures.

Security and stability: In addition to being able to sail in calm water, a good captain must be able to steer his ship to safety in rough weather. When angry voices rise, there must be a voice that calls for restraint and calm; when confidence is eroded, there must be someone to build it up again; and when distress prevails, courage must always take over. Security and safety are fundamental rights that our people and investors must enjoy in our country and we must provide them under all circumstances.

Although we are a peaceful country, free from tension, should tension ever filter in from outside our borders, we will quickly reassure people and face the looming crisis head on. We will reassert our confidence in our country by launching new projects or expanding existing ones. We will also instruct everybody not to cancel any planned events under any circumstances.

- Sustainability: Excellence for us does not refer only to the ability to deliver outstanding service, but to the ability to provide it on a sustainable basis. Just like in Dubai, development is taking place all over the world, so our vision does not aim at competing with development elsewhere, but at competing with the world's centres of excellence. Comparing ourselves with developed countries is both right and necessary because only in such a situation can we compete on a global scale and truly progress.

Our success is one of the reasons we are confident about ourselves and our abilities, and why people elsewhere trust us. In the past, we have sent our teams to leading international airports in order to learn from them, compare and study their experiences. Now, we are hosting delegations from the very same airports to learn from our experience.

Ranking ahead of world-famous airports such as Singapore and Hong Kong, Dubai International Airport leads forty of the world's best international airports according to a number of surveys.[4] Exceeding the expectations of customers is one of the most established standards of quality. If a passenger expects to pass through the airport in one hour and finds that he has managed to finalize everything in half an hour, this is quality service. If a person expects a government formality to be processed within two days and finds that it is processed in one day, this is quality service.

The road ahead

People's expectations have no limits and are like a revolving door. People are always looking out for the best and the easiest means, and we must always surprise them with first-class services. Those who expected airport formalities to take half an hour now expect them to take just twenty minutes, and those who expect a government formality to be processed in one day, now expect it to be processed in just three hours. If I cannot constantly surprise the consumer by providing quality beyond his expectations, I will no longer be providing excellent service; in such a case, I will lose over a month what I have invested years to build.

Anyone who compares Dubai today with the Dubai of a few years ago will see the huge progress that has taken place. Nevertheless, the journey continues and the road ahead is long. The more we develop or upgrade, the more we will realize how much we have missed and still need to grow.

---

1 According to 2011 statistics, the number of tourists in Dubai exceeded 8 million.

2 Godolphin is the Maktoum family's private thoroughbred horse racing operation and was named in honour of the Godolphin Arabian. UAE Vice President, Prime Minister and Ruler of Dubai HH Sheikh Mohammed bin Rashid Al Maktoum is the driving force behind Godolphin.

3 Burj Khalifa is the tallest man-made structure in the world at 829.8 metres.

4 According to Airports Council International's October 2012 report, Dubai International Airport is ranked number four in terms of international passengers and number three in terms of international freight traffic.

CHAPTER TWELVE

Institutionalizing Excellence

Am I a good leader? I do not know and I guess no one else does. The people, the future and history will stand judge and I will accept their judgement no matter what it might be. Nevertheless, I am fully convinced that I am leading my people, not only on the right path, but on the only one available.

What is important is for me to always do what I consider my duty – to God, my conscience, my homeland, my people and my leader. I am therefore working today as if I were to die tomorrow and working for tomorrow as if I were to live forever. I am focusing all my potential, effort and time to serve my country, with the utmost courage, determination and power God has granted me.

One should focus on achievements, rather than titles and positions. I am at the service of my people and homeland. Assuming the post of Crown Prince of Dubai in the past was never my wish. I was asked to accept this position several times and each time, I asked to be excused; but when I was ordered to, I had to accept, because I could not possibly have refused an express request by my late brother, Sheikh Maktoum[1], may God bless his soul.

The same happened when he passed away and I assumed the positions of Ruler of Dubai, and Vice-President and Prime Minister of the United Arab Emirates. This is a heavy responsibility and I pray that God will help me fulfil my duties appropriately and guide me on the right path in doing so. Just like anyone else, I had parents who loved me and I loved them, and I have sons and daughters I love and hope they feel the same about me. I let the moment control my feelings – so that I am a leader when I lead, a poet when I write poetry, a cavalier when I ride my horse and a normal citizen when I meet the citizens of my country. I need little from my world; my prayer mat and water container are in my car wherever I go together with my work documents and my vision.

The Umayyad Caliph Yazid II[2] once said, "I was told that no one can rejoice for a full day and I have personally experienced this." I enjoy my work and believe no pleasure can be more rewarding to a leader than promoting the status of his country and improving the standard of living of his people. If, however, the Umayyad Caliph was referring to the days where there were no tasks to achieve, things to think about or decisions to take, I suppose he was not exaggerating.

My thinking is divided between the present and future, which means that part of it is dedicated to solving daily affairs and the other to that special vision looming on the horizon. A leader might see the light in the distance, but not see the tunnel leading to it; or he might see the tunnel, but not the light at the end of it. In both cases, he must be confident he is heading towards his goals, because they correspond with those of his country.

We live in a fast-changing world and face many challenges that we need to be aware of. We must be fully prepared to meet them and to respond to them as efficiently as possible.

If a leader insisted on a rigid vision, he would be assuming that everything would happen the way he expected. Since this is not always the case, a sound vision should take into consideration the unforeseen developments that could take place and should always include the right amount of pragmatic flexibility. The facts of today are not the only things subject to change; the vision and the way towards it are equally fluid. We could say that the larger vision is composed of several smaller ones, which, if executed successfully, lead to the success of the ultimate vision.

If the vision is far-sighted and involves interacting with transient factors, similar to those prevailing in our world today, realizing the vision 100 per cent is not a deal breaker and does not necessarily define the leader. What is important at the end of each stage where major progress is achieved, is that the leader should try to capitalize on the achievement and turn it into a launching pad for the next.

There are some areas in Dubai that are still on the road to distinction; but I can say with confidence that today, Dubai is recognized as an international centre of excellence. The next natural step is to institutionalize excellence in order to ensure its sustainability. A leader might be able to achieve his vision, but might not personally be able to guarantee its continuity in the distant future. How then can he ensure the sustainability of his work?

Institutionalization of excellence can do this. Today, many people consider Western democracy to be an example of an institutional state. As important as it might be for a leader to sponsor development, he must also support the institutions that maintain the latter. When communities reach a certain stage in their growth, the support and sponsorship of the leader become vital for consistent development. The development process must therefore be accompanied by building institutions, because civilizations are only as excellent as their institutions.

When we talk about Dubai's programmes for upgrading the performance of its government, we are not talking about a successful leap on any level, but about a development institution whose statute has gradually become an integral part of the functioning system of government departments.

Although the concept of quality might not have taken root in the thinking of all people, we can confidently say that it has become part of the work and social life for the majority of them. This explains why many managers are now talking about quality, when just a few years ago, it was the least of their concerns. Many government departments are, for the first time ever, organizing qualitative surveys to measure the public's opinion about their services, and designing their training programmes and cost efficiency plans accordingly.

Before the launch of such programmes, few people ever joined training courses, but everybody is doing so today. Moreover, these training programmes go beyond the traditional public sector courses, to include development of team spirit, customer service, efficiency and productivity. International conferences, workshops and seminars that regularly take place in Dubai allow civil servants the chance to meet experts and specialists in the fields of management, economy and technology.

They also allow them to make better use of all available human and financial resources, international relations and human interests; and transfer the experience and knowledge they acquire through attending such events to the next managerial level in their departments. Such an approach institutionalizes excellence in the public sector by promoting awareness among civil servants and motivating them to develop and keep pace with international progress.

The continuity of this concern calls for institutionalization, in order to consolidate it and secure full commitment to it. But the institution able to do it is neither legislative nor executive, because it might find itself in a situation where it cannot even guarantee its own existence.

What is the answer then?

The culture of excellence

Whoever speaks to a German industrialist is bound to discover one of the reasons behind the engineering excellence their industry is famous for. Exports are vital for a country like Germany and they are prospering because people trust the perfection of German goods, even though they are often more expensive than similar products from elsewhere. The most important reason for this excellence lies, however, in the fact that the German consumer expects high-quality domestic goods, and would not buy any of lesser quality – so companies have to take this to consideration or risk losing their domestic market.

Ever since the sixteenth century, German consumers have expected quality. When they asked Bismarck for advice, he said, "My advice to the younger generations of this nation can be summed up in three words: work, work and work." Since the latter part of the nineteenth century, work, production and quality have become a natural prerequisite of Germans and an integral part of their culture, philosophy and psychological conditioning. Even in remote German villages, you will see Germans competing to own the best, the most beautiful and most perfect things in life.

Although quality control and specifications in setting up institutions are imperative, the best way to institutionalize excellence lies in enshrining it in society. We must, of course, study the experiments of others and make them known, but the best way to maintain excellence is to develop it into a social conduct, so that it becomes an integral part of people's behaviour and psyche. We must make it an implicit part of trading, manufacturing and farming; in work places, entertainment centres, at home, in schools and everywhere else. It must become a part of people's lives, so that they will never accept anything less.

When excellence becomes a natural extension of people's psychological constitution, their links with mundane life will be severed and reverting to old ways will become symbols of backwardness and regression. If we want excellence to prosper, we must grow it inside people's minds. The much better, more secure and more permanent way to maintain excellence lies in linking it to the interests of people and their future, their performance and their social status. We cannot possibly stop the global race for excellence – we must join it. Once we do, we must invest in the right effort, time and tools. Everybody will then have a vested interest in protecting those investments.

People are intelligent and anyone who tries to sell an inferior service at the price of an excellent one will have no place in our market. On the other hand, those providing quality goods and services will see a growing number of loyal customers, and their businesses will prosper alongside. If we extend this concept to schools, clinics, restaurants, airlines and other means of transportation, the same is bound to happen.

The German consumer imposed quality on goods suppliers and service providers, but this does not mean that Germany has no quality control institutions. There are hundreds of such institutions and a strict federation for quality control made up of some 80 million Germans. Who can shut down an institution this large, challenge it or prevent Germans from exercising what they consider their sacred right – that of obtaining quality?

We Arabs are four times as numerous as the Germans. Who, therefore, can prevent us from exercising our sacred right to enjoy quality in everything?

Leading development models

Development in Dubai complements that of the UAE, and the nation's growth complements that of the GCC countries. Consolidating all these levels of expansion will unify the development of all Arab countries, which we consider our strategic economic gateway.

As I have always said, our achievements are not only for our own benefit, but for that of our Arab brethren as well. I am quite happy that our brothers have come to appreciate and cherish our development experiment, and we are ready to provide our expertise in their expansion plans whenever we are asked to do so.

Nothing is better than admitting our mistakes, because we have suffered long enough from self-proclaimed 'infallible' people. The development models adopted in the Arab world were not efficient and one of the reasons for this might have been that some countries chose the wrong friends and enemies. Economy is the key to politics; we have friends in the West and in the East.

Generalization is the judgement of the ignorant. Many people forecasted that the UAE's federal system of government would fail because it lacked sufficient central power and is made up of seven different member emirates. It is only normal that such judgements are made by people accustomed to highly centralized state systems and that federal experiments are doomed if they lack a strong central power. We have, however, proven that experiments like ours are viable.

The existence of seven member emirates has reduced the centralization of power and consequently contributed to the prosperity of the federation in the economic, educational and cultural domains. Once again, the critics were proven wrong, and I am confident that decentralization, which some consider a serious mistake, provides a better chance for success.

The GCC[3] also provides an excellent model for coordination and integration. We wished the speed of the achievements of that model would cope with the aspirations of the citizens of the member states, and we also realize how closely our destinies are linked. However, I do believe that the GCC has travelled a long way down the road to success for the benefit of the region as a whole and I wish that other Arab countries could match this.

We could have achieved so much more in the Arab world, cut short the road to development and avoided the mistakes of others, if only we had put the interests of our people above all other interests. Nevertheless, what happened in the past has happened and cannot be changed, but we must learn from our mistakes. We must also know that there is no single development formula to fit all and no single way to implement it. Every country must choose its path after considering various models and setting its goals. Naturally, there are priorities and alternatives to consider, but the prime objective must always take centre stage; therefore, we must clearly define the goals of our development.

Some development experiments can be copied while others require a certain amount of flexibility. Some result from the accumulation of knowledge and experience. What is made in Dubai is not made only for Dubai. The experiment is not limited to the concept, but rather includes the rules and regulations, the tools, techniques and teams, and progressive steps forward. Dubai Internet City, on one hand, contributed to focusing Arab attention on information technology. Dubai e-government was suitable for copying and replicating in concept, general structure and tools, and was consequently replicated in seven Arab countries. On the other hand, the Dubai International Financial Centre will play a crucial role in upgrading the standards of our region's financial institutions and operations. This will reflect positively on the investment environment, business efficiency and the wealth of nations and individuals.

Our experiment in managing free zones has shown other countries the way forward. When Iran asked for help to establish similar zones, we dispatched sixteen delegations loaded with experience and expertise. Similarly, we have helped Lebanon, Syria and Jordan and will always be ready to put our expertise at the service of our brothers and neighbours, because their development complements our own.

Although it might be a time-consuming process, each model must be evaluated on its merits and adapted after modifications, to suit the local circumstances of each country. Our circumstances are different from those prevailing in other countries. Excellence or quality, for example, are great ideas that ought to be applied in all Arab countries, but there are local restraints in each country that make it difficult to act at a certain moment. Energizing the government sector, for example, is a very successful undertaking in Dubai and ought to be replicated in all Arab countries, even though there are common difficulties that obstruct countries from adopting excellence and quality.

There are no two different explanations for this situation. If we cannot share such experiments, then something must be wrong, either with the experiments themselves or with the circumstances. Our own experiments are beyond hypotheses; they are the basis of our work, the foundation of our success and the reason we believe that circumstances ought to change. If the vision is right and easy to understand, it is valid anywhere, regardless of the size of the country concerned or its population; but if it is wrong, it will fail wherever it is adopted. Implementing a certain vision might require more time than planned and the change needed might be deeper than envisaged, but these terms relate to the implementation and not to the vision itself.

In previous chapters, I discussed various elements of development and there is no need to repeat them here. But if I had to choose one single condition for a successful development process, I would say it is leadership. If the leadership is not committed to change, then change will not take place, the government sector will not be energized, and there will be no excellence, quality improvement or true development.

Most of the other conditions are simply tools or technologies that can be purchased or obtained one way or another. We have, for example, been urging the West to transfer technology to us, but is there in fact any technology we need and cannot actually purchase from the East or the West? We established Dubai Internet City in just one year, when we did not have the funds needed to finance the undertaking. Although the venture required highly advanced technologies, we did not face any difficulties in sourcing them. In some cases, we were able to use technology from companies now located in Dubai Internet City (some of which are multinationals at the cutting edge of the world's most advanced technologies) and in other cases, we were able to procure the technology.

If by transferring technology we mean, for example, that of manufacturing multi-purpose orbital satellites, let me ask you: what would we actually do with this technology if we obtained it right now? If, on the other hand, we are referring to techniques of horticulture, this is something we are always on the lookout for. Horticulture is a 183.5 billion-dirham-a-year industry in Holland (this is equivalent to US$50 billion). Moreover, our weather and land are suited to certain aspects of horticulture, and some of our local varieties have been famous worldwide for several hundred years.

We must always be practical, realistic and optimistic, focusing on our strengths, our unique features and on using tried and tested expertise. If the necessary elements for adopting a certain development model are not available, we should not use this as an excuse to procrastinate. Even taking the shortest step forward is better than sitting idle. Such a step could be about the concept of the model and not the model itself. If there are any obstructions, let us at least try to develop the idea.

Sometimes, just talking about excellence inspires an urge to reach some degree of excellence. Just talking about energizing the government sector might trigger a debate on the subject, leading to an acceptance of its merits and a desire to adopt them. Transferring the experiment then becomes easier and quicker to implement... as a matter of fact, this is how we started.

Transferring development

The shortest way to revive the fire of Arab imagination and unleash Arab potential to initiate a renaissance – one whose fruit can rival those of the past – is to work for the future. Lamenting the past is a waste of energy that we can turn into positive energy through work and acquiring skills. The Arab nation has all the ingredients for becoming a great nation; it only needs the 'development moulds' capable of achieving this goal – one that is the right of our people.

Dubai may not yet have – or need – the technology for manufacturing and launching satellites, but has several other successful development experiments ready to be put at the disposal of Arab countries. Consider the following:

- We welcome some 6 million tourists every year and provide them with quality services in more than 270 hotels, offering more than 25,000 rooms and 6,500 hotel apartments. The Arab world lies in the world's most important tourism area. It is the birthplace of the most important civilizations and a treasure trove of archaeological sites, monuments and cultural diversity. The most intact ancient Roman cities are not located in Italy but in Libya, Tunisia, Syria, Lebanon and Jordan, and these countries have as much Roman and Greek archaeological treasures as Greece and Italy.
- Where cheap energy is available, heavy industries can yield large profits; but if it is not available, let us focus on trade, niche farming and tourism. Let us market our sun, sea, sand, cuisine, traditional souks and our legendary Arabian hospitality. Such services create large numbers of jobs and benefit individuals, companies and governments alike. The cost of holidays in traditional tourism destinations is on the rise, and

tourists from the GCC countries and other countries of the world will opt in ever-increasing numbers for more economical destinations.

- We have a number of advantages over traditional destinations, including the all-important aspect of security. If we Arabs can provide the right facilities, we can host up to 200 million tourists a year. This is not an unrealistic figure because Italy and Spain jointly host up to 100 million tourists a year. If the average per capita tourist spend is US$1,000 (AED 3,670) for example, we could expect receipts of US$200 billion (AED 734 billion)!
- Dubai's GDP stood at US$37 billion (AED 136 billion) in 2005, but what would such a GDP amount to on a pro rata basis for a nation of 330 million people? US$6,000 billion (AED 22,000 billion)! Such a figure would leave only the US ahead of us (with an estimated GDP of US$12,370 billion or AED 45,400 billion), and would be near to the combined GDP of the world's second and third largest economies, Japan (US$3,867 billion or AED 14,192 billion) and Germany (US$2,446 billion or AED 8,976 billion).
- The profits of the Emirates group stood at US$708 million (AED 2,600 million) in the financial year 2004/2005, so how much would the operational profit of all Arab airlines amount to if they had all adopted the same operational principles? What losses would we have saved ourselves if we did? Money which could have been put to very good use in developing the Arab nation...
- There are some 80,000 members of the Dubai Chamber of Commerce and Industry. If the total number of members registered with all Arab Chambers of Commerce and Industry numbered 1 or 2 million, imagine what all these businesses could do? Cooperation, projects, job opportunities and unlimited wealth for all!
- We are not facing the unemployment problems that others do because we utilize our human resources to their full potential. Our projects will provide all our university graduates with jobs for the next ten years. Some of the graduates will be sent overseas for further studies while

we will train the rest. We have plans and ventures to help the younger generation establish companies and businesses in all fields.

We know that this will cost a great deal, but whatever we are going to spend on training and qualifications is a major investment in the future. We do not know of any better way. We do not expect everybody to become prominent businesspeople, but a single excellent idea implemented in an excellent way can have a huge impact on society. One outstanding company can provide tens of thousands of job opportunities and generate billions of US dollars. The Finnish mobile phone manufacturer, Nokia, is one such example, but there are scores of similar examples around the world.

They say in the management world, "If you think the price of training is high, consider the price of ignorance." The population growth rates of Arabs are among the world's highest and most are at the right age for training for the labour market. In twenty years, Arabs will number some 425 million and some of us think this number will be a burden on our budgets and society, and predict a bleak future with poverty and problems.

People are a blessing if they are productive and a burden if they are not. If Arab governments manage to train their workforce and provide them with the required skills, the future will be bright.

Developing individuals is the secret of developing societies, because when you train an individual, you're training a society. The important thing is that we should not despair, but rather start from some point in a well-planned manner. This is not an impossible mission because we have already done it here and everybody else can do it.

Why do we seek excellence?

The best way to answer the question, "Why do we seek excellence?" is by asking another: "Why should not we seek excellence?"

I started this chapter with the statement that excellence in development is an integral concept of civilized society. Excellence is also an integral part of our heritage and religion, which urges us to seek perfection in everything we do, to commit ourselves to high moral values and to be gentle when we deal with others. God says in the Holy Qur'an, "When a courteous greeting is offered to you, meet it with a greeting still more courteous or at least of equal courtesy. Allah takes careful account of all things."[4] There are numerous examples in Arabic literature, poetry, proverbs and in our heritage, as well as in stories related verbally by the elderly, that serve the same purpose.

Popular proverbs are important because they can be spontaneous expressions of deep consideration and serious messages. One such Arab proverb says, "An expensive product is worth its price." This simple message reflects a deep understanding in ordinary Arabs of the value of quality. It is more expressive of the virtues of quality than anything else I have read to date.

Excellence means quality, so why do not we want quality for our children, our youth and ourselves, whether we are in the UAE or elsewhere? In the long run, the cost of quality is not higher than that of low quality, and results in excellent services and better rewards. Although these are important reasons for seeking quality, there are more important ones.

Today's world is very different from that of the 1970s. An importer or anyone seeking a service can sit behind a computer, examine a picture of what they want to buy – wherever it might be in the world – and compare its price with that of scores of similar products or services. It is also possible to read an independent evaluation of the quality of that product or service, order and pay for it, in the comfort of your office, home or even from your car – and in a very short time.

Computer skills were not a prerequisite to obtain a job ten years ago, but are now no longer a bonus in the race for excellence, or even an option. They have become essential, just like knowing how to read and write, and those who do not master these skills are unlikely to find themselves a good job. Things have even reached a point where some people find it difficult to write with a pen and some of us – I am one of them – follow world news and developments through the Internet. Computers have become, for some of us, the ideal medium to establish a dialogue with customers, relatives and friends; a wide window to knowledge, information and expertise; and consequently, essential tools in our quest for excellence.

Geographical borders are not as important today as they were ten years ago because the new economy does not recognize them. Customs barriers do not have the same significance today as they did ten years ago. Yesterday's technology is not today's and today's technology is readily available at lower cost, so that it can be used to manufacture better quality goods in a more cost-effective way. Even consumer preferences and expectations are different today.

Consumers nowadays can identify quality goods and services; they know their rights and refuse inferior products, because they can always obtain their requirements elsewhere. If our children can source their requirements through the Internet, just think what businessmen can do with it. The most important feature of the new economy is that it allows consumers to compare and select. It provides them with options that never previously existed in such large numbers. This is happening today, so you can imagine what the picture will look like ten years from now!

In the age of the Internet, fast communications and ample choice, countries and companies are no longer able to compete in the global marketplace with anything but high-quality goods and services, because quality is not a luxury anymore. Governments are no longer able to force their citizens to buy domestic products in order to bolster the national economy and cannot force them to accept lesser-quality service in national airlines.

Consumers now want the best value for their money and if local companies cannot respond to this, they will just turn to other sources.

In the past, governments used to ban imports altogether or impose prohibitive customs duties and taxes on them, leaving their citizens with no other choice but to buy local goods and services. This is no longer possible in the age of free markets, open economies, speed and excellence.

Neither the Jebel Ali Free Zone nor Emirates Airline competes with counterparts in developing countries, but they compete on an equal footing with the best in the world and provide an even higher quality of service. Our airport, hotels and companies are doing the same.

The value of the 'Made in Germany' or 'Made in Switzerland' mark, if not worth billions, is priceless. The mere existence of these words on any product assures consumers everywhere that they are not only buying the product, but investing in the perfection that goes with it. The benefits of such a mark would remain out of reach, even if you organized the world's largest advertising campaign over several years.

We want to reach a similar situation, where the mark 'Made in Dubai' will be synonymous with excellence, not only in the Gulf region and the Arab world, but all around the globe. We are heading towards industrialization and want the goods we manufacture to bear a prestigious mark, with all that it involves in quality and commitment to international standards and specifications.

For these reasons and scores of others, we will always seek to achieve excellence and be world pioneers, not because these are personal goals, but because they are an absolute necessity for us to keep moving forward. If we cannot achieve this, it is only a matter of time before we start falling behind and lose the race. This not only means we will be at the end of the herd of gazelles... it also means we will be closer to the jaws of the lion!

---

1 Sheikh Maktoum bin Rashid Al Maktoum (1943–2006), the former Vice-President and Prime Minister of the UAE, Ruler of Dubai and Sheikh Mohammed's eldest brother.

2 Umayyad Caliph Yazid II or Yazid Ibn Al Walid Ibn Abdul Malik (701–744) reigned for six months and died in office. Yazid II was the son of a Persian princess who had been gifted as a concubine to Caliph Al Walid I.

3 GCC or the Gulf Cooperation Council is a political and economic union comprising Saudi Arabia, United Arab Emirates, Kuwait, Qatar, Oman and Bahrain.

4 Sura Al Nisa, v. 86.

Part V

THE ROAD TO THE FUTURE

CHAPTER THIRTEEN

The Race of Nations

In 2001 I said that the road to pioneering and success was still open to serious, dedicated people working for progress. During the following five years, we have added much to our previous achievements in Dubai, and have launched and completed a large number of mega projects, within the framework of a vision that extends up to the middle of this century. Nevertheless, I am still convinced that we have not achieved more than 10 per cent of our goals and are still, in fact, at the starting line.

Whenever we talk about the future, we should be talking in terms of challenges that lie ahead. Our ambitions are big and we anticipate even bigger challenges. Our ability to overcome these challenges depends on our capability to plan, work and feel optimistic and confident about ourselves, our potential and our capacity to reach our goals. Great challenges make great nations and when I look back to the past and then to the future, I am convinced we will overcome these challenges and succeed. We did so in the past and can certainly do so again.

For more than thirty years, the ability to overcome challenges and quickly accommodate all sorts of changes has been one of the most important strengths of the United Arab Emirates. We must adopt quickly with the various and rapid changes ahead; we foresee huge challenges and should therefore move comprehensively. It is crucial for us to maintain our momentum in developing and upgrading education, human resources, social participation and engagement, parliamentary representation and the leading role of the private sector.

We must also energize the role of the public sector; promote transparency at all levels and in all industries; expand investment incentives to reach beyond the free zones; incubate small and medium enterprises; upgrade finance programmes of new projects; fight corruption; simplify procedures; and introduce excellence as a basic requirement in all our activities.

Strategically organizing human resources, fostering a better investment environment, upgrading infrastructure, reforming the legal structure, strengthening the partnership between the public and private sectors, polling public opinion and showcasing Dubai as an international centre for excellence and creativity are basic, ongoing prerequisites. We must continually study the best ways to improve and reach innovative solutions that promote efficiency and enhance benefits.

Our society is prone to many negative influences that we do not always pay attention to, even though they have substantial impact on the individual, corporate and social levels. We must rid ourselves of these aspects as quickly as possible by encouraging positive behaviour, promoting honesty and upgrading performance. In the long run this will lead to positive results, enable us to optimize our resources and contribute to providing an environment that promotes excellence and creativity.

Overcoming the challenges of a new century in a new millennium calls for fresh methodologies and innovative approaches. This, in turn, calls for change. Change also indicates a change in mindset; the ability to understand the language of the New World and convey our message, standpoint and goals, in a clear, simple and frank manner. If we achieve this, the world will understand us and allow us to promote better cooperation between nations, eliminating sources of misunderstanding and focusing all our efforts on development.

Our goals are strategic, as are our plans and aspirations, so that the change we are talking about should respond to all of these and match them. During the last thirty years, we have acquired vast experience in finding innovative solutions to resolve the problems in transitioning Dubai into the modern age. We must, however, be prepared to face the most sensitive and complicated challenges that still lie ahead. This calls for all of us to shoulder our responsibilities, be realistic in our analyses and decisions, distinguish between facts and illusions, and set our goals and priorities precisely, in order to mobilize the resources needed to implement them. If necessary, we must equip ourselves with a strong will to overcome the impossible and walk the extra mile to recognize reconciliation of opposites at any time and on all levels. If anybody thinks we are hopeful of a miracle, I would like to remind them that challenges often trigger miracles.

Peace

When we talk about the future we will be talking about peace – but we still need to be realistic. The nations of this region are dispirited by military conflicts and tension, and seek peace and stability. Most of the negative aspects nevertheless still remain in one way or another. Clearly, the reason for this is that there is not enough resolve to secure peace and build stability.

I believe that the world's major powers are directly responsible for the sorry state of affairs in the Middle East, because they are the only powers capable of imposing or implementing the resolutions of the international community. They are also the only ones capable of leading the Middle East towards just and comprehensive solutions. I do not know of any other region in the world that has been as deeply affected by international competition over the past 100 years.

The world's major powers dealt with the issues of the Middle East with the mentality of a broker, and not as a neutral third party. They sought solutions that served their immediate interests, instead of proposing fair and just solutions, in line with international laws and resolutions.

However, we now see a positive change materializing, with serious attempts on the international level, mainly in Europe, to reach the roots of the problem. We therefore believe that a just solution for the Arab–Israeli conflict may still be found, while a way to save our neighbour Iraq from its tragic conflict may also be found.

Achieving sound development and political reform while establishing social justice will cure another aspect of the problem. I believe the international effort against terrorism should move simultaneously on two fronts: direct security interface and efficient treatment of the causes, which I earlier presented.

While I consider the major powers to be directly responsible for the present situation in the Middle East, I am not exonerating the Arab parties concerned from their responsibilities. Through their actions and policies, some of those parties give others excuses or alibis, and do not correctly read the facts of the present international system, while others continue to let their sentiments control their decisions.

Avoiding such pitfalls lies in applying reason, justice and logic; focusing on the broader picture instead of getting bogged down by detail, and concentrating on the survival of the nation rather than its destruction. It also lies in rejecting terrorism outright and giving precedence to the interests of the nation over those of individuals. We do not know of anything in particular we have gained from all the wars Arabs have fought over the past fifty years, but we know that the First and Second Gulf Wars drained the finances of the region, delayed the implementation of its projects and postponed development for years.

Outside our region, things do not look any better or less complicated, which means that mankind still has a long way to go before enjoying global peace. We now hear some people who have regressed to the mentality of the nineteenth century, referring to a struggle between civilizations and religions, while I believe they ought to talk about a struggle over interests. Other people are talking about hostility between Muslims and Christians – they obviously have not read the Holy Qur'an.

Some people still believe they can achieve peace through military victory – these people did not read history correctly. There is no such thing as permanent victory or defeat in the history of nations. World War I ended with a great victory, but World War II was fiercer and deadlier than all the wars the world had previously witnessed. After four major wars and numerous mini wars, the Middle East does not look any closer to peace today than it did ten years ago. We learn from this that the one who makes peace is more important than the one who wages war.

Some people believe that wars are also the best way to jolt weakened economies. They obviously do not understand the importance of peace yet. While government spending in military activities or even the aftermath of these activities boosts economies, sustainable development has proven to be more profitable. Government spending no longer drives today's economies; individual spending does. Wars instil fear and anxiety in people, naturally leading them to restrict their spending to the bare minimum. This is one of the reasons why pearl trade in the Gulf region collapsed.

Our regional and international policies are neutral and well balanced, based on the principle of avoiding involvement in international conflicts and alliances. We are not afraid and do not intimidate anyone; we do not exercise pressure and do not yield to any pressure; and we do not interfere in anybody's affairs nor allow anyone to interfere in ours. We entertain good relations with everybody and have no ambitions of power anywhere in the world. We want to keep all our bridges open and earn everyone's trust. Although we are strongly committed to peace, we know that true peace will only result from genuine, collective efforts.

All that we wish for is to resolve conflict according to international law, restore rights to those who have been denied them, provide all mankind with equal opportunities and lift the siege imposed on Arabs. We can then focus our attention on developing our countries and pursue our aspiration for excellence. This is our greatest goal and any talk about threats facing the region in the future will not hinder our march. We do not believe that the language of war can solve any problem that dialogue cannot solve, whether it is the dispute between Morocco and its Arab brother Algeria, or between the Emirates and its Muslim neighbour Iran.

The most important features of the UAE's development experiment are not limited to its sustainable and optimistic approach, but extend to its ability to maintain optimism and trust when prevailing tensions hit their peak and negative thinking dominates. We are full of hope about the region's future because we are optimistic about the chances for peace. We believe that the region should enjoy sound security and stability as fundamental factors for consistent development which will project elsewhere considering the region as a whole is one of the most important sources of oil and gas.

Although we are deeply optimistic and our hopes are high, we must, at the same time, always be realistic. One of my dreams is to visit Jerusalem and pray at the Al Aqsa Mosque. Every time I feel that I am about to realize that dream, peace is shattered and the dream moves further away.

There was a time we believed that the twentieth century would become a century of global peace, especially following the huge suffering mankind endured as a result of the ferocious wars it witnessed. Unfortunately, that century ended as the bloodiest mankind has ever known. We cannot postpone development indefinitely, until peace puts an end to a very long era of tension, the likes of which the region has never known in modern history. This calls for adopting all sorts of alternatives in our development plan.

Democracy

Democracy for us signifies the right to choose. My father never imposed his opinions on us, and brought us up on the principle of freedom of choice. I am convinced that this is the right way to deal with people, because persuasion is more effective and more sustainable than all other methods of enforcement.

Freedom of choice is one of the basic rules of democracy. If democracy was imposed by decree, it will end by decree. If we forced society to adopt a concept such as democracy before allowing it to debate the very concept on the largest scale possible, we would be pushing society into free fall. If we want to impose democracy on people, we would be breaking the most important principles of democracy. It is obvious then, that democracy should not be used as a modern weapon to threaten, interfere or segregate.

Democracy should not feel threatening to us, because we have been practising our own brand of democracy for a very long time. What is possibly frightening are the social, economic and political consequences that could arise if a nation's leadership shelves or ignores the real problems that exist, and opts for a Western-style, democratic system, without properly preparing their people.

If properly practised, democracy has many benefits and advantages, but it is not a magic potion to cure all kinds of social, economic and political ailments. It does not generate jobs, protect us from recession, guarantee the election of the best candidates, nor prevent wars or absolutism. Some regimes act as if democracy is a mere process of polling voters, while others, in the name of democracy, violate international law and perpetuate atrocities. There are also those who conveniently forget their electoral promises.

Our presence in this region is not temporary and our nation was not born recently. We have been here for thousands of years and intend to remain here for many more. Our conscience, nature, and conscious and subconscious minds store the accumulated memories of our past civilizations, as well as their heritage and customs. If a man abandoned all of that to become a western democratic, then he will lose his original identity.

We are part of the large international community in our aspirations, goals and cooperation, but just like all other nations of the world, we are unique and have our own special lifestyle. Democracy is not a 'one-size-fits-all' garment. What was suitable for the West at a certain stage of its political and social evolution might not have been suitable for the East at a different stage of its evolution; and what is suitable for nations in the southern hemisphere might not suit those in the north.

I am not against a democracy that is chosen by the people based on proper evaluation and true conviction. I am also not against any system that maintains security, stability, rights and moral values; or a system that allows me my freedom of expression, my personal freedom and the right of exercising my humanism, religion, customs and traditions.

We must, however, affirm that adopting a western democratic political approach is not simply a licence to obstruct true reform and development, enshrine injustice, hinder institutionalization, oppress individual freedoms and ignore human rights. Few countries are faithful to their democracies, come peace or war. Even fewer countries continue to protect the civil rights of their citizens when danger threatens or when subjected to economic or security pressures.

The fundamentals of democracy guarantee the individual's right to go against the masses and say 'no' according to the dictates of his conscience. They also guarantee his right to call for change, when people cling to tradition out of fear and frustration. Such principles could be quite difficult, if not impossible to implement during turbulent times and especially during wars. But this scenario is not limited to democratic regimes and whoever believes otherwise does not fully understand our way of thinking.

Arabs are living in a region of the world that has seldom known any long-term peace. The world 'seldom' here does not mean twenty, 100 or even 200 years, but refers back to the Second Crusades more than 900 years ago. Every time a war ends we find our region on the verge of another, and every time we emerge from one dark tunnel, we find ourselves entering another.

Whoever wants Arabs to have democracy must wish them two other things: permanent peace that allows us to divert military spending to civil causes; and sound development, so that our people have a vested interest in guaranteeing the continuity of peace.

Globalization

In my opinion, globalization creates an international economic platform that provides opportunities to achieve high levels of integration in commercial, financial and service-oriented activities. It also involves sincere commitment to certain principles and regulations that will introduce massive changes the world has never known before. Countries vary in their economic sophistication in terms of flexibility and capabilities. This directly reflects on their abilities to cope with the rapid developments of the global economy. Some countries might therefore face less acute challenges than others.

There is much discussion – and many articles are published each day – about the globalization of the world's economy. We are ready to deal with this and benefit from the opportunities it offers us. We will embrace whatever is in our interest, and use it for our own benefit and that of others, while excluding anything that is not in our interest. We will never be the weak player and would rather lead with open minds in order to benefit from and positively interact with the dynamics of this change. We are quite convinced with our ability to distinguish between what we do and do not need, and also what we can and cannot benefit from.

We, like other nations of the world, are no longer isolated from globalization. Nevertheless, we have our own convictions, principles and values that govern our progress and the way we deal with the global environment that is seeping into all countries.

Based on a perceptive understanding of developments in our world, Dubai has formulated its own response to these changes, while at the same time maintaining our identity, particularly in terms of our religious and moral values. This is because we are a civilized nation with high moral values and achievements that have spread to the rest of the world in many different ways.

The world has benefited from our remarkable exploits in science and all other fields of knowledge. Our history in Andalusia and other parts of the world is full of great minds who have introduced many new practices. Many of our scientists excelled in medicine, mathematics and astronomy, and the world is still indebted to them for the wealth of knowledge they provided.

That is why I believe we are ready to deal with all the new economic environments and systems, and other innovations without any difficulty. Our vision is solid, our means are sound, our goals are clear and we are ready to interact with the new changes. In our drive towards modernization, we are more enthusiastic about the new economy than most other nations, especially in terms of knowledge and information technology.

We look at globalization as a new road to development and not as an objective in itself. We accept the process because it is suited to our long-term development strategy. We believe that globalization is the best available medium for the success of this strategy, its development and its integration with the global economy.

Globalization is a new course for the development race between nations, and an opportunity for the UAE and other countries to contribute to making the world a safer place to live in; a world with greater mutual understanding and more productivity. We believe we have the right plans, visions and resources to prove our worth in the globalization race.

Interdependence between countries is on the increase. No country in the world can claim it is truly self-sufficient in all respects, and this includes the United States, with its huge industrial and financial might. The world, and not any single country or any alliance of countries, is the home of globalization. There is therefore no escape from keeping pace with globalization and interacting with its many positive aspects and offerings. We cannot be oblivious to the rapid and constant developments around us. This is not in the interest of any country.

I wish the globalization drive would take the interests of all countries into consideration: to promote development, protect our endangered environment, reduce economic, financial and technological gaps, and make a major contribution to reducing poverty by putting an end to famine, illiteracy, disease and all the other problems the world has failed to properly address. If globalization does not take all this into consideration, it will not win the majority support that is so crucial for its success.

The UAE has been a member of the World Trade Organization (WTO) since 1996 and is an old hand at free trade. We are ready to meet the prerequisites of the new economic age within the framework of globalization and the WTO's treaties. We are also ready to meet the requirements of the global economic turnaround until the middle of this century and beyond. Waiting for events to take place before dealing with them has never been our choice in the past and will not be so in the future.

There is no single economy or economic bloc that can present itself as an alternative to the global economy, nor claim its ability to monopolize development or technology, or close the gates of the world's economy. Eventually, interests will overcome whims, permanent benefits will overtake temporary ones, and countries will overcome their present fears in favour of a general conviction that creating true development opportunities requires an international market, exceeding the size of anything available today.

The way to achieving this is to remove economic barriers between nations, and to consistently strive to make the global economy a more integral and efficient one in a healthy, competitive environment. This requires sincere cooperation between all countries, regardless of their allegiances, philosophies and political systems. Hunger, disease and illiteracy, and not other civilizations or religions, are the eternal enemies of mankind. We must cooperate to eliminate these problems. Economic development is the key to all other disciplines of development. One of the most important factors for a successful economy is for people to have money to spend and energize the economy. This requires providing jobs, security, justice, peace and securing people's rights and economic interests.

Skills

Only mankind, and not machines or capital investment, can conquer the impossible. God blessed us with the knowledge of this fact, enabling us to scan the future and exploit the creative powers of our society. I am convinced that teaching our children in the same way we did yesterday is in itself perpetuating a new kind of illiteracy that no longer has a place in any society that wishes to join the global race.

Success in this race calls for educating new generations – who believe in God and realize their commitment to their nations – in all kinds of modern disciplines, to qualify them to compete globally in various fields of modern science. We can only achieve this by upgrading our education systems, gearing our teachers with the latest tools, using modern technologies in education, and providing a dynamic academic environment that promotes scientific research, innovation and creativity in compliance with an advanced, practical and all-inclusive strategy that prioritizes education as a vital pillar of our nation's comprehensive development plan.

So when we are forecasting our future, we are speaking about people with adequate educational qualifications, competencies, potential and independent ways of thinking. We are developing sustainable local expertise to build up a steady supply of human capital, capable of dealing efficiently with the challenges that lie ahead and providing us the highest levels of quality and productivity.

We must supplement our elementary education with capable institutions that enrich knowledge, promote creativity, encourage innovation and initiatives, motivate ambitions and prepare managerial talents to lead society and business.

The prime objective of our present and future development initiatives focuses initially on the social dimension, and consists of introducing comprehensive plans to enrich our human capital and enable our citizens through education, training and support.

Preparing for the future involves, first of all, training our young citizens to lead the development process, driven by a sense of their absolute duty to maintain our economic evolution. This will encourage them to place their dynamic potential at the service of our society. We have a wealth of young talents, and it is the responsibility of each and every sector of society to nurture them. This can only be done through proper education, training, support and encouragement; and by scouting for special skills and talents, while also nurturing creative initiatives.

Excellence in development requires excellence in managing our human capital. We expect our young citizens to excel in trade, industry, management and all other economic activities. Meanwhile, we will continue to attract skilled and talented professionals who specialize in critical disciplines related to the new knowledge-based economy.

We have implemented a number of major projects and are on our way to implementing some new, strategic ones. We are, however, aiming to establish an economy based on the largest possible number of SMEs. We want to expand markets horizontally, increase opportunities available to these companies and allow them to flourish. We want to build our economy from the ground up by helping SMEs evolve over time, so that they provide a base for a sound economy.

Many people do not like economic risks or cannot handle them, so the government must nurture entrepreneurship by fostering initiatives, removing obstacles that prevent them from turning their ideas into successful enterprises, and establishing tools and programmes to finance their ventures.

We expect our mega projects to generate hundreds of subsidiaries and to help in creating a scenario that encourages young people to establish their own businesses. This approach will promote more investment in both the traditional and new sectors of the national economy, mainly in IT, communications and e-commerce industries. We will extend sufficient support to these start-ups and will provide them with expertise, knowledge, advice, and financial and marketing support. After these businesses pass the phase of establishment, our support will be pro rata to their performance.

The vision and the future

The final goal of any vision conceived by a leader is to serve his people. Relying on a limited group of people to outline and develop the details of such a vision will result in the kind of visions people do not need. For a vision to meet the interests of people, we must know what they want because they will be the prime beneficiaries of that vision.

We must therefore undertake field surveys in the streets, in company offices and in shopping malls, and expand the scope of the dialogue and consultation to the point where it covers the largest possible number of people from every walk of life, whether they are involved in trade, manufacturing, services, management, education or anything else.

In the next stage, the leader must consult senior local officials and a select group of experts and specialists from the most prominent and dedicated universities, research centres, companies and organizations. The consulting body should cover all aspects related to the vision, including the economic, social and political planning from all around the world. We should then provide them with the outline of the vision and allow them to freely discuss and provide suggestions. Accordingly, the leader may reconsider his vision and amend it if necessary, before revealing its details to the public and converting its elements into a plan.

Consulting and conducting surveys are essential tools to ensure planning consensus. Once consensus is achieved, the vision becomes applicable. We must walk this extra mile to give our development plans the human depth it deserves, as well as the necessary regional and international dimensions most suited to acquire support for our development aspirations.

We need to study and understand the new concepts and rapid changes taking place around us, before drawing a clear work plan that will accommodate all these factors and help us attain the best results. This will also help us benefit from the experience of others in developing our own capabilities in modern and social sciences and philosophy, thus promoting our competitive powers and securing the right conditions for success and prosperity.

People are the asset of any vision – they make it real. And people will not allow the vision to materialize unless they are convinced about its validity, and certain it will meet their expectations and interests while remaining practical, clear and simple. Everyone must believe that his opinion counts, and that he or she must contribute to the vision. This will generate a sense of ownership; only then will the citizens and expatriate residents of Dubai become a genuine part of the emirate.

This is the background for our vision for Dubai until 2010. It is a systematic, ambitious and comprehensive economic vision, essentially focusing on people. We believe that we have the power, resources and determination to realize it the way we want. We can summarize the objectives of my vision as follows:

- Increasing the GDP of the Emirate of Dubai by 100 per cent.
- Increasing the average individual income in the emirate by 100 per cent, to become one of the highest in the Middle East.
- Expediting the diversification of economic resources by:
  a. Raising the contribution of manufacturing and services in the emirate's GDP to 70 per cent.
  b. Raising the contribution of IT and intellectual property activities in the emirate's GDP to 20 per cent.

c. Raising the capacity of Dubai International Airport from the present 24.7 million passengers a year to 70 million passengers, and launching Dubai World Central International Airport with a capacity of 120 million passengers, creating a combined potential of 190 million passengers.

d. Raising the number of tourists visiting the emirate to 15 million, and providing the necessary support for expanding the fleet of Emirates Airline, launching new destinations, increasing the number of shopping centres, hotels and tourism and also entertainment facilities.

- Allocating a crucial role to young citizens in implementing the vision, through focused initiatives that will enrich our human resources and contribute to supporting entrepreneurship, and qualify nationals to shoulder their responsibilities in the development process.
- A commitment to keep pace with social and economic development, in order to attain an ideal social balance, promote the role of women, assert social values, promote tolerance and fight prejudice, according to the principles of our religion, Arab values and heritage.
- Promoting our international competitive powers by:

a. Developing the services industry to ensure its continued excellence.

b. Implementing a number of new strategic projects on schedule.

c. Focusing on developing the IT and communication industries.

d. Promoting Dubai's status as an international financial and investment centre, by equipping it with a highly advanced infrastructure capable of attracting major international investors, facilitating the flow of capital, establishing an efficient regional financial market and encouraging the repatriation of Arab assets.

e. Helping the private sector prosper by eliminating obstacles hampering its activities, expanding Dubai's markets, promoting the efficiency of the public sector and developing promotional programmes and festivals that are capable of increasing production, trade and tourism.

Although some of these goals are quite ambitious, I am well aware of our strengths and weaknesses, and I am not proposing anything that is beyond our capabilities. When I first presented my vision for Dubai Internet City and e-government, many people said that implementing such projects within such a short time was impossible, because we were embarking on a totally new road that no one in the region had taken before.

I maintained my optimism and we managed to realize all our goals as planned, with the help of a dedicated group of work teams and expert managers who were conscious of their responsibilities and roles, and successfully fulfilled the difficult tasks they faced until the project was completed.

I am happy with the results we have achieved but as I always say, this is just the beginning and realizing the targets of Dubai Vision 2010 requires us to keep up the team spirit that has always marked our work in Dubai and has been one of the most important factors of our past achievements.

We also have to embrace the role of the information economy and transform our society into a knowledge society. Only then will creative ideas become one of the most important elements in achieving success. They are also a practical test that will ensure we are heading in the right direction. We will know we have realized our goals when the world admits us as full members of the international community and when we provide our Arab nation with a successful example to follow.

We have a strategic long-term vision based on the Dubai 2010 vision, that covers the period up to 2050. In time, we hope a new vision will emerge to take Dubai beyond 2050. The most important features of this vision are to achieve a high rate of economic growth, to increase our participation in global trade and investment activities, to make an active contribution to strengthening and developing the Federation and to deepen our economic reach in the UAE, the GCC, all other Arab countries and the rest of the world.

This vision is based on consistently developing Dubai's modern and traditional economy, achieving maximum cooperation between the public and private sectors, and promoting Dubai's status as one of the world's most important trading hubs and transit centres. It is also based on turning the UAE into an international centre that attracts hi-tech industries. This will be done by training capable candidates in evaluating and managing industrial projects, and efficiently marketing their products in the international marketplace; and by making use of the opportunities provided by the shift of multinationals to more efficient, lower-cost production centres.

The next economic cycle will be marked by new economic disciplines that require high levels of specialization, efficiency and concentration. We are working on providing the ideal environment for Dubai to become an international hub for such multinationals and to professionally deal with new tools and methods that can increase our competitive edge, in a world endowed with an economy that knows no borders, barriers or protectionism. We are also aiming at:

- Making the UAE the world's favourite hub for finance, business, trade, tourism, insurance and services over the next fifty years.
- Making the UAE one of the world's leading countries in the information economy, virtual markets and an international IT centre of excellence. This will be achieved through the development of national human resources and concluding strategic partnership agreements aimed at attracting the world's largest players in the industry. Included in this will be those dedicated to the development of new technologies and creative new ideas, in addition to highly specialized experts and talents.
- Making the UAE a Gulf, Arab and international centre of excellence for training and human resources development, fully capable of dealing with new technologies and communication systems.
- Making the UAE an international pioneer for the new economy.
- Emphasizing security, stability and the rule of law throughout the country, and using all suitable forums to dissipate any wrong impressions about investment in the country.
- Promoting the country's regional and international role as a unique centre of excellence.

The central world

Most major economies of the region we generally call the West have reached maturity and share high levels of technology, integration, efficiency, exploitation of resources and adherence to common economic practices. Although there are still many differences between these countries – some of which are very important – they constitute a distinct economic bloc. A similar bloc exists in the Far East with countries such as Japan, China, Hong Kong, Singapore and others.

Between the East and the West, there exists a middle economic bloc including more than thirty countries, most of which do not belong to either of the above blocs in their development levels and economic characteristics. This third bloc includes countries such as the GCC, the Indian subcontinent, the northern Gulf countries, Central Asia, the Near East, Turkey, Cyprus and both East and North Africa. This bloc forms what is now known as the Central World Economic Zone.

Similar to the Western and Eastern economic blocs, the countries forming this zone vary in terms of their economic growth, political systems, social and ethnic structures and human, financial and natural resources. However, from whatever angle we look at this central world, we are bound to discover an entity that constitutes about a third of the world's population, amounting to some two billion people. A closer look will also tell us that the overall GDP of this world amounts to US$1.5 trillion (AED 5.5 trillion), which is just 12 per cent of the United States' GDP of US$12.4 trillion (AED 45.5 trillion) and 40 per cent of Japan's GDP of more than US$3.8 trillion (AED 14 trillion). The value of the visible trade of this bloc, on the other hand, stands at only US$700 billion (AED 2,570 billion).

One of the most important benefits of studying the history of nations lies in the fact that it may provide us with information about what may happen to those nations in the future. The central world region is the birthplace of all heavenly religions, the most glorious empires of the ancient world, and some of the most important centres of civilization, thought, science, trade and architecture.

History is the record of humanity; therefore, two or three centuries pass in the blink of an eye. Soon, the central world will hopefully assume its position as the cradle of civilization and retrieve its golden age.

The elements that helped this region reach its golden age 1,000 years ago still exist today. The nations of the central world that created civilization are the same today, and their present-day nationals are no less intelligent and innovative than their forefathers were ten centuries ago. The bottom line is that, if it adopts the right development formulas, nothing in the central world is preventing it from developing economically to the point where it can match the development levels achieved by the two other blocs. We can easily imagine the huge potential of this region, when its share of the world will not be restricted to hosting a third of its population, but also a third of its wealth.

Is there any evidence to support this possibility? In the UAE we have in place the infrastructure of the new economy, we have upgraded the quality of our services and we are keeping pace with radical changes in the global economy. We are actively, efficiently and quickly interacting with these changes in order to fulfil the major goal of promoting the status of the UAE on all levels and its role as an international gateway for finance, business, trade, technology and tourism. That is why we believe that what we have achieved so far, and what we will achieve in the future, is proof enough that our model can be successfully replicated in all the central world countries.

The furthest country from us in the central world is just a four-hour flight away and all the nationals of those countries have been our brethren, neighbours and partners in building civilization and trade for hundreds of years. Dubai offers the countries of the central world a practical and tested development model, one that can be amended to suit the local conditions and the needs of the individual countries concerned. We also believe that this huge bloc can consider Dubai as a positive agent of change, because we are an integral part of it.

Dubai used to be a station along the East–West trade routes, but it is now a gateway to the four corners of the world. The countries of the central world need an economic capital, and we believe we can fill this role because we have the necessary infrastructure, and because we are actually playing part of it already. We will keep developing our role in the future, until Dubai becomes the economic capital of this world.

This statement is supported by several facts. The number of flights between Dubai and Hyderabad and Mumbai exceeds that between Hyderabad and Mumbai themselves. The number of flights between Dubai and the UK (92 weekly) equals that between the UK and all Arab capitals. We are operating 49 flights a week to Australia and will keep expanding our network, which covers more than 80 different destinations. A large number of the 24.7 million passengers using Dubai International Airport do so as a transit point to other countries for trade, business and managing projects. Companies operating from Dubai deal with traders from India, Pakistan, Africa, the Arab countries and scores of others. Many multinationals serve the central world from Dubai, through warehousing, distribution and after-sales centres.

A quick glance at Dubai's trade performance between 2001 and 2006 will show the deep changes affecting its structure, and that we are heading in the right direction. Just a few years ago, Dubai's largest trade partners in imports were traditional major trading countries such as Japan, the United States, Germany, the United Kingdom and France.

Yet, by 2004, China led the pack (US$4.9 billion or AED 18 billion), followed by India (US$4.6 billion or AED 17 billion) and Japan (US$2.7 billion or AED 10 billion). The US, Germany, the UK and France trailed in that order. At the same time, we find that most of the twenty leading countries in exports and re-exports to Dubai come from the central world region, led by India (US$2.1 billion or AED 7.7 billion), followed by Iran, Iraq, Yemen, Saudi Arabia, Indonesia, Turkey, Pakistan, Somalia, Tanzania and so on.

I believe that Dubai does not only provide all those countries with an excellent economic centre, able to meet their development needs, but also provides them with the hope that they, as well, can achieve excellence in development by mustering the same optimism, determination, self-confidence and courage that helped Dubai. Those countries have all it takes to succeed: natural and human resources, finance, talents, skills, potential, a free-enterprise spirit, the ability to generate wealth, large consumer markets and others. What these countries lack, however, is an awareness of their strengths and a commitment to use them to shape their own new golden era.

The Arab world

A smaller world lives inside the central world, but is different from the East and the West in most of its structures, growth levels and economic relationships. This world is, however, distinguished by having all the necessary ingredients to build another new golden age. It also has two of the four most important factors needed to build strong nations, a common religion and a common language, although it still lacks the other two factors, which are a common flag and strong leadership. I am, of course, talking about the Arab world.

There are no civilizational, cultural or ethnic gaps to speak of, nor are there the major differences in customs, aspirations, tastes, social and consumer behaviours we tend to find everywhere else. Nevertheless, the Arab world lacks sufficient awareness of the risk of isolation, and other related future risks, resulting from the constant and gradual move by neighbouring countries to growing economic and consumer blocs. The Arab world is at risk of becoming an isolated island devoid of the trade and economic bridges that used to link them to other parts of the world.

Where is the vital Arab economic depth today? What is the value of inter-Arab trade? What happened to the Arab Common Market? There is no proper regional cooperation, no proper Arab cooperation and no proper Arab cooperation with neighbours or the rest of the world.

Some Arabs have tried to remind us of our shortcomings and weaknesses, as if they were the only ones who knew these facts. However, we no longer need to indulge in negative energy. On the contrary, we need positive energy, we want to be optimists, we want to realize economic visions and we want to win. We need people who can remind us of our strengths and show us successful development projects that turn visions into realities.

The gazelle and the lion example at the beginning of this book is not directed only to the people of the UAE. It is addressed to Arab people everywhere. The West may be ahead of us economically but not in terms of civilization.

Most of the problems Arabs face today are similar and any solution in one Arab country can work in another. What cannot be solved now can be solved in the future, but the most important thing is to start, because the ideal time to start a development process is always immediately.

We in the UAE did not have much when we started, but thanks to the wise leadership of Sheikh Zayed, we now have everything advanced countries aspire to: sound trade, manufacturing and farming sectors, and excellent security and stability. The countries that led us in development and prosperity in the past have fallen behind us and we are excelling just like the most advanced countries.

Critics may argue that Dubai is a city and the UAE is a small, oil-producing country, and that they can therefore achieve their goals easily. But sound vision, efficiency and perfecting the techniques of using financial and human resources have nothing to do with size and oil. Many oil-producing countries cannot come close to us in their growth rates. A small and highly profitable company is much better than a huge, unprofitable company.

Cities such as Venice, Genoa, Marseilles and Pisa, among others, were the pillars for the West's Renaissance during and after the Crusades. Cities like Dubai, Hong Kong and Singapore are now realizing the highest growth rates in the world, while a handful of other cities, including New York, London and Frankfurt, are leading the economies of their respective countries and controlling the flow of funds and investments in most other countries of the world.

I have previously said that it is about time the Arab dream had a chance to awaken and become a vision and a reality. I believe that this nation is destined to become a great one. All our past years of regression are but a blink of an eye in history. If this sounds optimistic, it is; but it is an optimism based on facts and not illusions. We have all we need to engage in a great development process, but this does not mean a thing right now.

The pillars are strong but they are lying down, the doors are large but they are closed, the walls are high but they separate us from each other. We therefore need to find leaders capable of raising those pillars to the sky, opening the doors to the world and breaking down walls that prevent Arabs from meeting one other and participating in development. Can we do it? I am sure we can, but we first have to regain the pioneering spirit we have lost in leadership and in society.

An Arab leader must be loyal to his people and his country and committed to realizing their dreams and ambitions based on a clear and modern vision. In social terms, we have to get rid of all obsolete aspects of our life and engage in dialogue with other civilizations. It is equally important for us to remove all kinds of misunderstanding and promote cooperation and friendship with the people of the world, while striving to pioneer in manufacturing, technology, trade, education, culture and all other related fields.

Let us forget all the ado surrounding us, ignore threats, discussions about war, tension and hollow words about conflicts between different religions and civilizations. Our region is on the verge of an economic boom on a scale it has not witnessed for more than 1,000 years and it does not need an exceptional effort to perfect the recipe for making great nations: security, the rule of law, sound economic decisions, careful planning and implementation, and putting an end to blaming others for shortcomings for which we only have ourselves to blame.

Seeking the approval of others is one thing and seeking the interest of the country is another. Our tendency to lose great opportunities in the past can be treated by availing ourselves of the present ones and providing the right conditions for making even greater ones.

The policy we have to adopt is to prepare ourselves for the great economic race – and then go on to win it.

EPILOGUE

Achieving success requires taking the right decision at the right moment. Such decisions were at the very foundation of Dubai's success during the latter half of the last century and we are confident that the decisions we are taking now will make Dubai even more successful in the future. Each one of us has the right to dream and to have our own visions, goals and time frames to achieve them. All leaders dream, but only a true leader can turn a dream into a vision and a reality.

Vision is the way to true development and is also a matter of courage and conquering the impossible. It is believing in our ability to achieve our goals; a matter of having clear objectives and realizing them with determination, efficiency and speed, never pausing until our children see their country competing with the world's most successful economic centres.

I believe that I have provided sufficient evidence in this book to say that achieving excellence is a realistic goal, not only for Dubai, but for the whole of the Arab world. I also believe that upgrading the role of the United Arab Emirates from a regional to an international economic power is a natural development. In order to keep the momentum of the economic prosperity our country is currently enjoying, and move forward, we need to reduce our reliance on natural resources and to maximize excellence in quality services and tourism. We must focus on developing a knowledge economy and human resources to reach the high economic growth rate we aspire to.

We do not want to find ourselves, anytime in the future, pawns to a single source of income, and will always observe the need to diversify and avail ourselves of all suitable opportunities. Until recently, we were content to catch up with others, but we were so successful in this that we have moved beyond that scenario and are now aspiring to a pioneering role.

We want that pioneering status in full and will not settle for anything less. We want it not only for our own sake, but for the sake of all Arabs. Catching up with others comes at a price, but attaining a pioneering role has an even greater price. Our forefathers taught us that pearls do not float on the sea, waiting to be scooped, and that we have to dive to great depths to harvest them. We must therefore be prepared for anything and everything, no matter how hard this might be.

The UAE has proven that it can turn ideas into realities, as shown by the Jebel Ali Free Zone, Emirates Airline, Dubai International Financial Centre and scores of other successful projects. The future will see an exciting world – one in which only those who have the right tools and attitude will attain a pioneering status. These tools are flexibility, innovative ideas and an ability to respond quickly.

Every country wants to be a pioneer and each one is prepared for the great race – one that is likely to become the greatest race the world has ever known. I have often been asked where the development going on in Dubai today will lead us and my only answer is, "To victory."

This, however, is not the only answer. There are others related to the education we have enjoyed, our motives in life and what we want to achieve. If my motive is the progress of my people and my country to the status they deserve, at what point should I stop? What progress would we have achieved if we had all stopped?

Some people have asked me, "You have a vision for the development of Dubai, but have you ever asked yourself what will happen to that vision if you are no longer here?" A big question maybe, but perhaps one with a small misunderstanding behind it. Although it is true that I am managing, planning and contributing to the implementation of my visions, I want everybody to know that I could not have achieved anything without the trust of my brothers and their constant support. I also could not have achieved anything without my dedicated teams and the support of the private sector.

I never achieved all this success on my own; every single person working in the government, every single person working in the private sector and every single person, wherever they may be, who has helped us achieve our goals, did. I must, however, give the private sector credit and say that the government would not have been able to achieve so much without its support. So our success is that of the private sector first and then of the government.

If anyone bragged about the goals they have achieved, chances are that they will not be able to achieve any more. When we are at the beginning of the road there is no time for bragging. What lies ahead of us is much, much more than we have done to date.

What will happen to the vision if the visionary goes away? I have asked myself this question and found the right answer: "Nothing will happen, because my vision of Dubai has become Dubai's vision of itself." The vision will go on regardless – Dubai will continue to exist and continue to develop itself.

Other people with mixed feelings of scepticism and confidence would ask me whether I was convinced that Dubai would compete with international centres of excellence in places such as the United States, Europe and Japan. My answer to those people is always the same: "I have no doubt that Dubai will be able to compete." I am convinced about this, even though it is not our final goal.

We are not only racing others, we are racing against ourselves and time. Life presents a limited number of opportunities that must be taken and not lost, and development is an ongoing process that cannot afford delay or hesitation. Dubai is part of the UAE, the UAE is part of the Arab world and the Arab world is part of the rest of the world.

Because the horizon has no limits, a vision cannot have any boundaries. The closer you come to the horizon, the more the boundaries extend. A visionary must match these new boundaries with new aspirations in order for his country to provide magnificent opportunities for mankind.

We will keep pushing our vision forward. Those who succeed us, their successors and all those thereafter until the end of time, will forge ahead along the same road. Will that be the end of the vision itself? Of course not, because my vision today is not the same as the one I developed twenty years ago. A vision cannot remain intact after being exposed to new technology such as e-commerce, the Internet and globalization. If it does it will become frozen in time, without any flexibility or horizon, and will not be able to cope with modernization or people's changing needs.

When vision changes, the work plans and methods of implementation also change. All the teams I am managing use modern development methods, and have quickly absorbed expertise and accumulated knowledge. They have put all this at the service of our goals, resulting in higher productivity and achievements.

I want our team leaders and senior managers to acquire all the knowledge and skills they possibly can, in the largest number of fields possible. When I transfer one of these people to a new sector, he will take with him his accumulated expertise and skills, and add new ones. This is an ongoing process – the acquisition of skills never stops, just as providing constant guidance, increasing efficiency and reducing time, effort and cost are continuous processes.

What is the end result of all this?

If time went in a full circle, we would have accomplished what we have achieved during the past twenty years in just five years. But since acquiring skills never stops, we will double what we have achieved during the past twenty years in the coming five years.

If this does not give you an idea about what we have in store for the future, then let me summarize it one final time.

Life consists of a number of opportunities and great opportunities do not come knocking on people's doors. Whoever wants such opportunities must grab them when they arise, for his people and for himself. We have to be powerful, strong-willed, determined and willing to grasp such opportunities, so that we do not have to scavenge the leftovers of lions.

I will never abandon one opportunity and wait for another. We have not reached the goal we are striving for. What you see now is nothing compared to our vision… just tiny parts of what lies ahead.

We will build a great monument on these foundations and it is my wish that other Arab countries will follow suit so that we can develop the Arab world into a world of excellence. The hand of the UAE is reaching out to join the hands of its Arab brothers, so take it and let us start building together.

I know the road to development and modernization is difficult; I know that it is long and I also know that the next stages will be even tougher and longer. But I have faith in God, I believe in my people, in the wisdom of our leadership and the future of our nation. I am confident we will realize our goals. Our vision is clear, our road is paved and the clock is ticking. There is no more time for hesitation or half-baked goals or solutions. Development is an ongoing process and the race for excellence has no finish line.

رؤيتي

التحديات في سباق التميّز

محمد بن راشد آل مكتوم

MOTIVATE